Helping Children Cope
with Separation and Loss

FAMILY FUTURES CONSORTIUM
35 Britannia Row
Islington, London, N1 8QH
TEL: 020 7354 4161 FAX: 020 7704 6200
A NOT FOR PROFIT ORGANISATION

Child Care Policy and Practice
Series Editor: John Triseliotis
Director of Social Work Education
University of Edinburgh

Published:
Adoption and Race
Black, Asian and mixed race children in white families
Owen Gill and Barbara Jackson

Specialist Fostering
Martin Shaw and Tony Hipgrave

Long-term Foster Care
Jane Rowe, Hilary Cain, Marion Hundleby and Anne Keane

Children in Care Revisited
Pamela Mann

In and Out of Care
The Experiences of Children, Parents and Social Workers
Mike Fisher, Peter Marsh and David Phillips with Eric Sainsbury

Social Work with Black Children and their Families
Shama Ahmed, Juliet Cheetham and John Small

Groupwork in Adoption and Foster Care
John Triseliotis

Direct Work with Children
A Guide for Social Work Practitioners
Jane Aldgate and John Simmonds

Conciliation, Children and Divorce
A Family Systems Approach
John Howard and Graham Shepherd

Adolescents in Foster Families
Jane Aldgate, Anthony Maluccio and Christine Reeves

Helping Children Cope with Separation and Loss

Claudia L. Jewett

B.T. Batsford Ltd
in association with
British Agencies for Adoption and Fostering

To the Giver of health,
who provides for the return
of love, hope, joy and meaning;

and to Fran,
whose dying began it all

© 1982 The Harvard Common Press Inc., 535 Albany Street, Boston, Massachusetts 02118, USA

First published in this edition 1984
Reprinted 1986, 1988, 1989, 1991, 1992, 1993

Printed and bound in Great Britain by
Redwood Books, Trowbridge

for the publishers
B T Batsford Ltd,
4 Fitzhardinge Street, London W1H 0AH

ISBN 0 7134 4707 9

Foreword

This is a book that has long been needed by anyone who has dealings with children, whether as parents, social workers, therapists, teachers or doctors or just as caring people. It is written by an experienced American child therapist, but no-one should be daunted by the image that may conjure up. Claudia Jewett writes clearly and directly and gives a multitude of examples and practical advice, so that the book is both easy and enjoyable to read.

Such books are badly needed in Britain. We have many which discuss the theoretical aspects of grief, of separation, or of loss, but all too few which convey in simple language exactly what the ordinary person or the professional worker can do to help. When it is a child who is suffering, the task is as painful and difficult a one as any adult can encounter. Claudia Jewett fully acknowledges this, but sets out to show how vitally important it is that the help should be given, and offers some tools with which to undertake the work.

That is where this book is such a boon: it is practical and down-to-earth, and one can see that the methods suggested have been tried and tested. There are examples of children losing parents through death or divorce, or through disrupted foster-placements, followed by discussion of the dilemmas facing the adults in explaining to the child, and then suggestions of how actually to do it; there are examples of how children show, or repress, feelings of sadness, anger and guilt, followed by ways of opening up a discussion, exercises, games, and all sorts of unlocking devices to help the adult get through to the child. No-one who works with children could fail to find a helpful idea or to gain a better understanding of a child's pain. Neither could anyone miss the message of the importance of being honest with children, and not only honest, but explicit in a way that is comprehensible to a child. In a country where the tradition of understatement may be misleading to a child, where euphemisms, especially about death, are rife (e.g. 'I lost my father last year') and where folk-lore can be terrifying ('If you do that the bogey-man will get you') this message cannot be too often or too loudly repeated.

Claudia Jewett's work is based on a wide acquaintance with diverse schools of thought on both sides of the Atlantic. She draws on many people's thinking — about mourning and grief, about separation anxiety, about childhood fantasy and about child development — and incorporates the best of it in her discussion of the more practical aspects of handling the problem.

It is a hopeful book, since from her own experience the author shows how children *can* be helped, and can come through periods of grief or trauma, without being destroyed or overwhelmed by them. Much of the hope lies in outlining the help: nothing makes us feel so inadequate as when we must stand impotently watching someone else's suffering. If we can think of a way of helping we immediately feel more positive and this in itself probably conveys itself to the sufferer.

Claudia Jewett not only dispenses practical advice, but also helps us to gain more insight. She shares with us, for example, her understanding of children's ways of thinking. She illustrates the 'magical thinking' common to so many children ('Step on a crack, break your mother's back' or 'If I'm really good, Daddy will come back to us') and shows how some comprehension of what is going on in children's minds is an indispensable first step towards helping them sort out their pain, confusion and guilt.

This kind of understanding can be applied to any work with children, not only those who are suffering through bereavement or loss. There are lessons about how to help improve a child's sense of self-esteem, and how to improve relationships between parents and children, which are relevant in any context.

As in her earlier book *Adopting the Older Child*, Claudia Jewett makes all these tasks seem manageable, and makes the reader feel there is something she or he can actually do to improve matters. Need one say more, except 'Read on . . .'

February 1984

Phillida Sawbridge
Director, Parents for Children

Contents

Introduction:
Who This Book Is For

CHILDREN UNDERGO THE EXPERIENCE of separation and loss in dozens of ways—the death of a loved one and the divorce of parents are just two. There are as many individual situations as there are children—each with particular circumstances, personalities, and backgrounds.

Chances are, though, that you are thinking of a particular child as you read this. You may be in the middle of a divorce, entangled in your own pain and problems and yet worried about the effect it is having on your children. Or you may be trying to help a child who has had the terrifying experience of losing a parent to death. You may have recently moved to a new city, and be concerned at the changes you observe in the behavior of your children. You may be coping with a long hospitalization, or a separation because of military service, or the new experience of putting your child in day care—and you may have felt the need for help.

Parents are on the front line in these situations. They must live from day to day with their children's reactions to separation and loss—and the reactions are disturbing, upsetting, and frequently infuriating. Often devastated themselves by grief and pain, parents feel they must be a tower of strength and understanding for their children. Where can they turn?

Other adults, too, are involved either by choice or by circumstance when a child suffers a loss. The teacher, for example, must find ways to cope with a child whose behavior and school performance suddenly changes drastically. The doctor or nurse must recognize the reasons for physical changes ranging from apparent hyperactivity to an increased susceptibility to colds and flu. The counselor, minister, or social worker needs techniques to help a child understand what has happened and why. Even close neighbors, relatives, or friends of the family will need all the help they can find to understand the sources of the child's reactions in his time of grief. If you are involved in any way with children—as a lay person or as a helping professional—it is becoming more and more likely that you will find yourself dealing with a grieving child at some point. Because of divorce alone, studies project, nearly half of all children born today will spend a significant portion of their lives in a single-parent family.

What are the effects of loss on children? Psychologists agree that they are severe, lasting well into adult life if the grief is not resolved. Studies show that emotional distress in adolescence and adulthood—including depression, alcoholism, anxiety, and suicidal tendencies—is often linked with bereavement suffered in childhood. And the immediate reactions to the loss, as the child struggles through the two or three years that follow it, are no less striking. Fears for personal survival; separation anxiety; impaired ability to make emotional attachments; sadness, anger, guilt, shame, and despair; problems with control issues; drops in developmental energy; loss of self-esteem; and pessimism and feelings of futility are all to be expected in the grieving child.

*

What can be done? Until recently, most psychologists believed that there was no way to help mourning children recover from their painful encounters with separation and loss. In pre-adolescent years, Freudian theorists held, a child's ego was so undeveloped that it rendered a child unable to comprehend a loss, and thus unable to mourn it. In the early 1960s, however, John Bowlby's groundbreaking work on childhood mourning shed new light on the issues of attachment, separation, and loss. His theories prompted new observations of children affected by losses; and his most recent work, the three-volume *Attachment and Loss,* cites many studies that establish that children grieve as painfully as their elders.

Still, almost no attention has been paid to the help that can be given children in resolving their losses. With adults, it seems clear that the way others respond to the mourner is a critical factor in determining how well the loss is resolved. But adults are often reluctant to respond to children in mourning—or they simply do not realize that the difficult behavior they encounter can be directly attributed to grief, and that it needs their understanding, support, and attention.

Sometimes children are denied help after a loss because those around them discount its effect on them. Or sometimes the child's caretaker is so deeply concerned about the loss that he is unable to take responsibility for the child's feelings and confusions. Sometimes an adult who might help is reluctant to intrude into someone else's family problems, or fears that good intentions might backfire, actually hurting or damaging the child more. And all too often adults have no idea what a child needs after suffering a loss or how they can provide the help that is needed.

This book presents a practical plan for helping a child through the recovery process. It helps identify the specific forms of behavior one can expect in a child who has suffered a loss, and it shows how they arise from the natural grieving process. In each case it distinguishes the behavior that may immediately follow a loss from the long-lasting behavior that may appear regularly in a child who suffered a loss years before and never resolved it.

From my work with hundreds of children as a child and family therapist, I have developed techniques and simple props to help children understand and cope with their grief. I will describe them here, and I will explain their theoretical underpinnings so it will be clear why they work so well. As a parent, if you use these practical methods day after day, you will help your child progress through the work of mourning towards a healthy adjustment to the loss. As a helping adult who is not the parent—whether you are therapist, school counselor, teacher, day-care provider, doctor or nurse, minister, or friend or relative—you can use them in your encounters with the child, to support him in his grief and to minimize the chances that he will founder or reach an impediment.

Because the first problem is usually how to tell the child about the loss, we begin with a general discussion of how to convey the news, and a description of the phases through which the mourning child can be expected to pass. The first two chapters provide a background for understanding the specific situations described in the last four. In these you will learn particular techniques that can help a child through the strong feelings, difficult behavior, and confusion that follow a loss. Through examples and dialogues from a wide variety of situations, we will see how children can be brought towards a resolution of their grief and a readiness to get on with life.

This book deals primarily with the child who loses a family member through death, divorce, or one of a variety of other reasons. But you will find as you read it that the emotions described apply to many other losses that children encounter as they grow up. A change of school or neighborhood, the loss of health through accident or illness, the death of a beloved pet, the loss of self-esteem through a friend's rejection or a failure in school, the passage from one stage of life to another, even the dashing of a secret hope or fantasy— all are accompanied by grief. No matter how trivial a loss, the same process must be gone through each time, though the length and intensity of the experience will differ. And loss is a cumulative experience; unless the child is helped to resolve a major loss, even trivial subsequent losses will provoke similar stress. The techniques you will find here will be useful in helping a child to recognize and accept the way things are in any of these situations.

It is a crucial task that we assume when we listen to the cry of a mourning child. Our success depends on our willingness to involve ourselves with the child through a troubled and baffling time. The methods this book describes can make this task clearer and easier. The challenge is great, but the rewards are rich; these methods promise full and happy lives for the children you know and care about.

1.
Telling a Child About a Loss

EVAN'S GRANDFATHER HAS LIVED near to him since Evan was very young, and the two have grown very close, sharing jokes, secret codes, and summer fishing trips at the lake. Just as school is about to close for the year, Evan's grandfather suffers a fatal heart attack. Evan must be told.

Lisa Hunter stands at the window, her forehead pressed against the glass, listening to the shouts of her children playing in the yard. They will have to know that she and their father have decided to separate, but it is so hard to think about telling them.

Julie came to live at the Kendalls' two years ago, an angry, difficult child. Although Margie and Sam Kendall have tried their best to work things out with her, they feel as if they are getting nowhere. They've called her social worker, who has agreed to find another home for Julie, but they feel terrible about how the child will react. Now what?

Each of the adults involved with these children probably has two immediate questions: Who should tell the child? What should they say?

WHO SHOULD TELL THE CHILD?

In general, the news is best shared by the adult to whom the child feels closest; the history of trust, concern, and involvement that person has with the child will be important during this time of crisis. If the loss involves parental separation or divorce, the news is ideally conveyed by both parents together, so that each can make clear that their love, involvement, and acceptance of the child will go on. If a family member is dying, the news is best told by a parent; but if at all possible the child should be allowed to talk directly with the dying loved one, so that they can share their feelings and say loving farewells. (Medical staff and other family members sometimes mistakenly prevent this.)

If the death is sudden, the child probably feels the most protected if informed by a loving, close member of the family, preferably the surviving parent. When this is impossible and the child must be informed by another adult, try as soon as possible to reunite the child with a trusted adult—preferably a parent —who can repeat the news. The more directly conveyed the knowledge of a death, the less chance the child has to deny it and to avoid making the life changes that will resolve the loss. If the death occurs at a distance, or news of it is conveyed by strangers, the child's tendency not to believe it is much stronger.

When the loss involves a change of custody for the child —because of a move to a stepfamily, a change in foster care, or a parental relinquishment—the move should be discussed with the child, either by the caretaking parent or by another adult known and trusted by the child.

There are, of course, problems with these direct approaches. Imagine the mother who has only a brief hour to prepare herself to tell her children, on their way home from school with a neighbor, that their father has died. Struggling with her own bereavement and shock, she must not avoid seeing them or discourage their expressions of pain. Even in peripherally involved adults a child's loss strikes a deep chord, triggering strong feelings left over from past losses, separations, or rejections of their own. Partly to protect themselves against this painful personal upheaval, many adults will avoid talking to the child about the loss at all—which leaves the child confused, afraid, and unable to resolve his emotions.

The same thing can happen when a divorce or change of custody is to occur. Harry, who is leaving his family because of his involvement with another woman, would rather not tell his children himself of the impending separation. To assume the responsibility for the deep distress his children will suffer makes him feel guilty and unhappy. But it is essential that they realize his love for them remains as strong as ever.

Often the helping adult will try to protect the child from harm and pain by deciding to keep things as normal and pleasant as possible, acting as if nothing important has happened, and hoping that the child will not notice the loss. The adult may think that the child is too young, or too fragile, to handle direct information. Unfortunately, this decision joins family members in a conspiracy of silence that deprives the child of her right to confront and resolve her grief.

Children in this situation are at the mercy of adults; they are hard pressed to figure out what has happened alone. John Bowlby, whose work on separation and attachment has shaped our fundamental understanding of children and loss, believes that a child can resolve losses just as favorably as an adult, given the following conditions:

1. The child has enjoyed a reasonably secure relationship with his parents before the loss.
2. He receives prompt and accurate information about what has happened, and is allowed to ask all sorts of questions and have them answered as honestly as possible.
3. He participates in the family grieving, including funeral rites.
4. He has the comforting presence of a parent or adult whom he trusts and can rely on in a continuing relationship.

We can best help the child cope by overcoming our

reluctance to talk about what has happened and by learning how to ease the healing process.

If you must tell a child of a loss, here are some questions to ask yourself if there is time:

Do I feel guilty or anxious about what has happened? If I do, can I keep from pushing the child to deny his own hurt and anger in order to please me and prove me right?

Do I feel rejected or abandoned, unloved or alone? If so, can I keep from adding my own burden to the child's emotional response? Can I avoid making the child feel that he must fill the gaps in my life, take care of me, fill my needs instead of his own?

Am I relieved at ending a bad situation? If I am, can I avoid expecting the child to share my feelings? He will need to acknowledge and express his own feelings if he is to work through them.

Do I feel insecure about practical matters—monetary arrangements, living situation? Can I avoid laying these burdens on the child? The child may need to know some of the facts, but the solutions to these problems must clearly remain my task.

Do I blame someone else in the family for what has happened? Can I be honest but nonjudgmental with the child? He must not be expected to choose sides against another family member, especially against either of his parents.

Do I have expectations as to the right way for the child to react? If it is hard for me to let the child express strong feelings such as anger, sadness, and despair, I will need to find someone else with whom he can share those feelings.

If you are a parent, it's not easy to separate out these strong emotions in the midst of a great personal crisis. You don't have to deny your own pain. It's all right to cry in front of your child. In order to get the distance you'll need to be able to talk helpfully with your child during his distress, though, you may need to vent your own feelings to a close friend or counselor. This helps you avoid inadvertently using your child as a confidant. But if you find that you are unable to talk to the child without your own problems interfering, help the child to find someone else—a school counselor, an adult friend—to talk with. You must protect the child from your own pain by making sure that someone listens to him with a balanced, compassionate attitude.

If in your own pain and grief or confusion following an unexpected loss you say something that you regret ("Daddy isn't coming back because he doesn't love us any more," says Harry's wife), you can always go back and make it right. ("When I said Daddy didn't love us any more, I didn't mean it. What I meant to say was that he doesn't love *me* any more. He still loves you just as much as ever.") Children will accept you, and believe you, if you are honest with them about yourself.

WHAT TO TALK ABOUT

How to Tell the Child What Has Happened

The first thing to communicate to a child when you must tell her of a loss is, "You are not alone; I am with you." One of the best ways to do this is through touch. Hold a child who trusts you on your lap, or soothe her with long strokes or a rocking movement. A counselor can put an arm around a child's shoulder, easing the tension that builds up in her head, neck, and shoulders; and even an adult who is not close to the child can establish non-intrusive contact by reaching out to touch her arm or her knee. Your physical presence, if you are caring and compassionate, can do more than words to show that she will not be abandoned.

If possible, begin talking to the child of things that she has experienced or noticed already. "You know that Mommy has been very tired lately and that she has needed to go to the hospital several times." "You know that Daddy and I have not been getting along well. You've seen us being very angry with each other, and you've heard us fighting." Or, for a change of caretaker, "You and your mom and dad have not been getting along too well lately." To begin with the child's experience makes it harder for the child to deny her own thoughts and feelings—which is easy to do if an adult simply hands over an adult explanation of what is happening.

To begin this way also gives the child permission to trust her own observations—to sense, "I am the sort of person who can figure out what is happening." This lays an essential foundation to the work of healthy mourning.

You may have had unwritten rules in your family that children should not be "nosy" about the affairs of their elders. When you tell your children about your decision to divorce, you should deliberately relax these rules, encouraging the children to voice questions about your reasons and observations about what has been going on in the family. If the questions are too personal to handle—or if the separation hinges on sexual matters inappropriate for discussion with children—you want to avoid implying that these things are "none of your business." Instead, you might say, "That's an okay question, but I feel private about the answer and I really don't want to talk about it."

In some families, children are discouraged from making critical observations or remarks about their parents. Here, too, the child needs your assurance that it is all right to have noticed that things were not going well. This tie to reality will keep the child from assuming that the loss is his responsibility. Children are very quick to "edit out" of their minds the part that parents have played in a separation. Corroborating the things that the child has noticed sends one more reassuring signal that the child is a thinking person, able to make sense of his own world.

Next, include the adult reality, the facts of the separation or loss. "The doctors say that Mommy is very sick and that she may not be able to get well and come home to us." "Your daddy and I are tired of all the fighting. We have tried to work things out, but we can't find a way that is good for both of us." A working parent who must place her child in day care might say, "I need to work at a job during the day. That helps me to be happy." Or a social worker might say, "You and your mom and dad have all tried hard to be a family to each other but it just isn't working."

If the loss comes with no forewarning, you should convey the facts in as straightforward a way as possible. "Today when Daddy drove to work he had an accident. His car skidded into a tree and he died." Or, "Mom and I have been having some grownup troubles lately. We have tried to work them out together. We didn't want you to worry so we have been pretending that everything was all right. But now we can't keep our troubles with each other a secret any more." The social worker who needs to move a child to another caretaker might say, "Your foster mom and dad are getting pretty old. They have trouble doing the things that they want to be able to do for you. We all think that it's time to get a different mom and dad to take care of you and help you." Or, "Your mom has been having a lot of grownup worries lately. She needs time to figure out how to take care of herself and take care of you. She will be going [to the hospital, to a counselor, for help with a drug or abuse problem], and she needs us to find someone else for you to live with while she is figuring things out."

Young children get their understanding of life primarily through their senses, not through their intellects. Particularly with difficult and emotionally laden information, then, it helps to tie the news to a sensory or bodily connection. The information will be more real to the child if it is conveyed through what he might have seen or heard. "When you heard us fighting you may have been feeling scared." "You probably felt that something was wrong when the principal called you to the office to tell you about the accident."

In addition, children process information differently from adults; and the way they process it changes as they get older. The earliest kind of thought process is often called "magical thinking," which begins in an egocentric stage when the child perceives that he is the center of the universe. His own thoughts, wishes, and actions, the child believes, cause what happens to himself and to other people. The children's rhyme "step on a crack, break your mother's back" is an example of magical thinking; many of us can remember mood stepping carefully over the cracks to avoid disaster, or stomping deliberately on them and then rushing home to reassure ourselves that the magic hadn't worked. (Interestingly, many of these memories stem from a time when we were giving up true belief in our power to cause bad things to happen, so that it became possible to experiment.)

Magical thinking is never completely eradicated in any of us, and it tends to recur in times of crisis, even in adults. ("If only I had a new job [or a new spouse, or a different hairstyle] everything would be fine." "If only I had insisted he stay home, it wouldn't have happened.") Young children experiencing separation and loss will almost always display magical thinking. ("My father left because I kept wetting my bed." "I got diabetes because I ate too much sugar." "I was adopted because I cried too much when I was a new baby.") The clear message that you must give to children in this situation is this: *It was not your fault. It was not because you were bad in any way, or because you were unlovable. There is nothing you could have done—or can do—to make things different.*

From magical thinking, children move on at about seven or eight to concrete thinking, which lasts until about the age of twelve. In this stage the child thinks in terms of "either / or." Good guys are good guys and bad guys are bad guys; there is little ability to deal with subtleties, ambiguities, or euphemism. (A Funky Winkerbean cartoon illustrates this concept best: "News bulletin: Today three armed men held up the First National Bank. Police are wondering how they could lift such a heavy building. Probably the fact that they had three arms helped.")

As with magical thinking, adults often cling to the simple blacks and whites of concrete thinking; and again, the pattern is most noticeable in times of stress. It crops up in complicated situations where blame must be assigned, in dealing with moral or religious issues, and in the political arena—and it shows up as "you always" and "you never" in countless domestic arguments.

Especially in the case of a death, the helping adult must be very careful to avoid using euphemisms or figures of speech when talking about a loss to a child in the concrete thinking phase. "We lost Grandpa," is all too easily absorbed by the child as literal information ("Where did you lose him, and why aren't you looking for him?"); and "She has gone to her eternal rest" can translate into a terror of going to sleep at night. Those who remark of an untimely death that "the good die young" are inviting a child to link good behavior with death and accordingly to act as bad as possible.

Even direct information can be misleading and problematical unless you reassure the child when you give it. "Is that going to happen to you or to me?" is the first question that will come to the child's mind, and children make all kinds of connections that would not occur to an adult. ("He kissed me the last time he was here, so I'm going to get cancer and die, too." "I can't sleep because I have to make sure my heart is beating.") Watch for the child's tendency to blame himself, and reassure him that death is a long way away for him and for you as well. If the child is very anxious, you can schedule a physical exam for both you and the child, so that the doctor can make it clear that nobody is in danger of dying.

It's never easy to break the news of a loss to a child; but there are several good books that can help you and the child open up discussion, find supportive words, and acknowledge the feelings that accompany the loss. Leone Anderson's *It's Okay to Cry*, about death; Janet Sinberg's *Divorce Is a Grown-Up Problem*; and *Young and in Foster Care*, by Noreen and Robert Burke will all be useful in their various contexts. (More information on these books appears in the bibliography to this volume.)

How much can a child really understand about death? Surprisingly, the evidence is that even a young child can conceive of death accurately, as irreversible and due to natural causes—but whether or not this happens depends on *what he has been told*. With any loss, John Bowlby points out, a child or adolescent can be expected to respond with any degree of realism only if he is given true information and the sympathy and support to bear it. This means taking care that the child understands that death is real and final, especially in the case of a child under the age of seven or eight. Because of the child's tendency to experience the world as a place of magical resolutions (as in the play world of "Bang bang, you're dead," where the victim gets up and starts playing again), a child at this age might react casually to the news of a death.

Even during years of magical thinking, children can be told honestly about death. Children are lucky if their parents use their early interest in a dead insect or animal to lay the foundation for a beginning understanding of death. A two-year-old may be incredulous at first when she is told that the dead bird will never come alive again, and that death comes sooner or later to all living creatures; but she is likely to accept her parent's word. And if she is told that when a pet dies it is natural to feel sad and to wish that we could bring him alive again, this too will conform with her own experience and show that her sorrows are understood. Again, it is important to stress the child's own senses and experience in order to make the death real. A young child will not understand the abstractions of words like "soul" or "life," but she will understand descriptions like, "The soft and warm part has stopped. There's no more eating, no feeling, no hugging, no hurting."

When you talk to a child about death, you must be completely honest. Answer the child's questions accurately—this means saying "I don't know" if you don't—and encourage the child to share her feelings by asking what she thinks. (This applies to questions about the afterlife as well; don't pretend to be confident about your religious beliefs if you aren't.) The child's trust, remember, has been severely shaken; you'll need to allay her suspicion that you may be withholding some fearful secret, some additional shock or threat. Likewise, you must be completely reliable in all your dealings with the child. Be sure she knows how long you will be around and in what capacity; and don't miss appointments you've made with her, unless you've been able to notify her personally of the change.

One very important function you serve is to give the child permission to figure out what has happened himself, to make it real again and again. This means letting him ask questions as often as he wants, and encouraging such questions by your responses. "I like how you're asking / thinking about these things," you might say, or "You must be wondering . . . ." Listen for statements that are hidden questions: "You hate me" ("Do you love me?"), or "Daddy didn't like me" ("Did he leave because he didn't like me?"). Unexpected new concerns may surface, also hiding questions: "Was I a good girl today?" your child may ask again and again, letting you know that she's making some connection between her behavior and the loss. Be sure to follow up on the child's statements and questions, making them more concretely apply to her own loss. "Jimmy's parents were having trouble over money, and then his father got a raise and everything's okay," she might say to you. "It wasn't just money that was the problem between me and Daddy," you need to point out, and go on to help her understand the situation clearly. In these cases, remember, very little that has happened is none of the child's business, with the exception of private sexual matters. A traumatic separation definitely *is* the child's business, and needs to be explained now to avoid serious repercussions later.

Encourage the child to remember and talk about the person who is gone. He needs to be able to have a picture in his room, to talk about his memories, and, in the case of divorce, he needs help in buying birthday presents, valentines, and the like for the separated parent. Strengthening positive memories is one of the kindest things that a caring adult can do for a child who has suffered a loss—and it can be done without intrusion even by someone who does not know the child intimately. ("I remember your mother always posted your report card by her desk at the office. She was so proud of you.") This is an important part of helping the child resolve the loss and make healthy adjustments to his altered world.

*

Can It Be Fixed?

Deep within every child is the fantasy that one day his parents will be gone. A parental loss makes this fear a reality, raising powerful fears for his own survival that must be recognized and relieved immediately. Most adults have learned that they can go on living after the loss of someone they depend on, but children have no such experience to fall back on. It can be devastating for a child to find himself in a strange world without the parents he has known to protect him. (This can happen not only when someone dies but also in the case of foster care or even day care.)

In this time of panic for the child, you should first reassure him that someone will take care of him and that his feelings are acceptable. "You may feel scared and sad and angry about what is happening," you could say, and tell him that you (or someone else) will be there to listen and to answer his questions.

Then come the hard questions: Can it be fixed? Will you get back together? Will I see them any more? Is she coming back? What will happen to them—and to me—now?

If the loss is a death, the two most important things to tell the child are first, that the dead person will never return; and second, that the person's body is to be buried in the ground or burned to ashes. It is very important that children be included in the funeral or memorial service for the dead person; if this is denied them, they are unable to experience concretely the fact of the death, and are left in the same unresolved situation as a wife whose husband is missing in action. The mourning rites mark the change that has taken place, and allow the child to see that many other people share in his sorrow and love for the lost person. They give him a sense of support and belonging when his security has been badly shaken, and they relieve his fear that he is to blame for the death. If a child is shut out of these services, he experiences damaging, scary feelings that he must have done something wrong.

Before the child goes to the funeral or the cemetery, explain the details of what will go on. There is no need to fear the child's viewing of the dead body, though you should never force him to view it or to touch it. In most cases, children are actually relieved to see that their ghoulish fantasies of the appearance of the dead are not true. After the funeral, you may see your child "playing funeral" from time to time. This is completely normal, and in no way disrespectful. Children integrate and master their life experiences through play, and such behavior merely marks the importance of the funeral in their lives.

If the parents have separated, questions are just as inevitable and as important. Make clear to the child that you have tried to work out your problems without success, and give a clear message that there is nothing the child can do (or could have done) to bring you back together. Be sure to underline the fact that the noncustodial parent is still the child's parent. Some things, such as how often the child sees that parent, will change; but children don't get divorced from their parents, you can reassure him.

Where the noncustodial parent will be living, when and how often the child will visit, and in what ways the parent will be available (by telephone, for example) are all very important things for the child to know. If these matters are not yet resolved, tell the child what will be happening in the immediate future, and assure him that you will let him know more as soon as it can be settled. Even though the family unit is being dissolved, continuity between parent and child is crucial.

If you must move a child into foster care, or from one alternate family to another, you may be hard pressed to tell the child what will be happening. Much of it may be beyond your control, in the hands of the court, the biological parents, or a particular alternate family. In these situations, share as much concrete information with the child as possible. If there is some condition the parent must fulfill in order for the child to be returned, let the child know what it is: "when your mom gets an apartment," "when your dad gets help so he does not do so much drinking," "when your parents can show that they know how to take care of you without hurting you," or the like. This takes away some of the mystery surrounding the move, and also lets the child know that he is not responsible for the separation.

If the move is in fact a result of the child's own behavior—in the case of an unmanageable or delinquent adolescent, for example—then you might make a contract with the child, spelling out the conditions of a reunion (if this is a possibility). You could explore the reasons for the unacceptable behavior with the child, for instance, and figure out other ways to meet his emotional needs. Parents might be sought who can live with the behavior, or the original parents might decide to change their minds and allow the behavior. Whatever the possibilities, in this case as in the others, direct information should be given as to what happens next.

If you are preparing a child for a final move into another family, you must also allow the child to have different feelings from your own about the move. Though you may think that this new family offers the best permanent situation for the child, remember that the child is faced with a lasting separation and loss. Honesty in this kind of situation is especially crucial. Don't say, "You'll just love it there"—during the time of grieving this will not be true. Don't promise, "They'll keep you forever"— what if it doesn't work out? In the case of an adoption, don't arrange "blind showings," where the prospective family has the chance to observe the child but the child is deceived about what is going on. All but the youngest children will figure out this ploy anyway; their trust in you will be shaken, and they will feel that they should not talk about their concerns with you.

Who Will Care for the Child?

"Who will keep me safe?" Whatever the cause of loss or separation, this is the fundamental anxiety of the child; it arises from the universal, primitive terror of abandonment and annihilation. Even in a crisis, when you do not know what will become of the child, it is important to promise that someone will take care of her.

Obviously, the child who continues to receive the loving, involved care of one of her parents will have the least chance of serious scarring from the loss, as long as the parent allows her complete freedom to mourn. If both parents have died, or if the remaining parent is unable to care for the child, the next best caretaker is someone whom the child already knows and trusts. The child can expect that such a caretaker will have her best interests at heart.

If a new family or caretaker must be introduced, several techniques can be used to make the change easier. For an infant or a very young child with little speech, the method of physically "handing over" the child to the new caretaker seems to work best. The Wilsons are delighted with Joy, the fifteen-month-old daughter they will be adopting. In order to help her make the transition from her foster parents, the Browns, they have spent part of two days visiting the Brown home, and Pat Wilson has closely watched Joy's routine. Sitting with Judy Brown at meal-time, she has smiled at Joy while the child was being fed. Midway through the meal, Judy passes the spoon to Pat and lets her take over the feeding. Watching her foster mother's face and body, Joy has a chance to see that it is safe in her familiar parent's eyes to take nurturance from this new person. This technique can be extended to include putting the child down for a nap, packing for the move, and other routines. An important action seems to be the actual handing of the child from one adult's arms to the other's, making the child feel that the familiar adult trusts the new one with his safety and well-being.

For older children, like seven-year-old Bobby, it helps if the child can experience either vicariously or by actual observation what the new situation looks like, sounds like, and feels like. Adoption workers have developed the technique of introducing a family by means of a book of photographs the child can look through. Bobby and his case worker sit together looking at such a book made for him by a waiting family. It reads something like this:

"This is the Jones family [picture of whole family]. They live in a white house [picture of the house] at the end of a busy street. This is Daddy Jones. He likes to fish, garden, and fix the house [pictures of him at some of these activities]. He would like another child to go fishing with. This is Mommy Jones. She likes to read, cook, and sing [pictures of her]. She would like another child to bake cookies with." The book goes on through the family, including the other children, pets, and typical family activities, and suggests how Bobby might share in these activities. The Joneses have wisely included a picture of the table where they eat (to show Bobby he can be nurtured at their house), the room with the bed where he will be sleeping (there is a place for you here), and the school he will be going to. Bobby and his worker can use this book and these pictures as the basis of a number of conversations to help Bobby feel less strange when he meets the Jones family.

Books like these are not limited to use with adopting families, however. With modifications to the text, they are equally helpful when a child will make the first visit to a distant parent, or when a stay with relatives is planned while parents must be away. In the Greene County Department of Welfare, each foster family is asked to make a similar book to be kept on file. At eleven one night, Peter Haney must make an emergency placement of six-year-old Becky into the Strongs' home. He stops at the office and picks up their family book. At the hospital where he meets Becky, he sits with her and says, "Your mom is sick and has to stay here for a while. She has asked me to take you to visit with some friends of mine. Let me show you some pictures of where you'll be going and who will take care of you." They read the booklet together, looking at the pictures. Becky is quiet, but Peter can tell from her face that she is looking at the pictures carefully, and she seems to be listening. He reads the short captions under the pictures, ready to answer questions if she asks them. The book has eased the shock of the sudden placement not only for Becky, who feels less as if she is being dumped off somewhere, but for the worker and the receiving family as well.

Lucky is the child who is not only given the chance to know something about the new family before a move, but whose parents also give their permission and blessing for him to be close to the alternate caretaker. The wise parent will not force the child to choose whom he likes best or which side he is on; the relinquishing parent gives the most precious gift when she can wish the new parent well. Parents effectively give this permission when they take the time for the child to make a gradual transition to the new family setting, by visiting often before the final move.

If the parent cannot give this permission in person, another helping adult can foster the feeling that it is all right to share one's affection with a new caretaker. Telling the child that the parents know this is a good choice for him, or would be happy to know that he was with this new family, makes it easier for the child to accept the new situation. One good technique for letting the child know that he can love a new family without giving up his parents' love is this candle ritual:

Holding one candle you might say, "When you were born, you had the gift to give love and to get love. This gift is like a light; it makes you feel warm and happy." (Then you light the candle representing the child.) "At first you got used to your mom. She probably cuddled you and fed you. You felt close to her." (And you put the child's lighted candle next to the unlit candle that represents the birth mother until it, too, lights.) "And you lit a love light with each other." Then you might go on, "Your dad thought you were really special. He played with you when he came home from work. He helped with your bath. You felt close to him [putting the child's candle next to the candle for the father until it lights] and you lit a love light with him too."

Then, depending on the situation, you might say, "Your dad and mom stopped loving each other. Your dad went to live in a different house. But his love light for you still kept going, and your love light for him kept going too." Or, "Your mom had an accident and died. The warm, loving part of her was gone [you might want to extinguish the candle or move it out of sight, depending on your religious beliefs]. You kept loving her even after she was dead, and your light stayed burning." Or, "Your first mom and dad had some grownup troubles. They had never learned how to take care of a little boy. It was decided that you would need to live somewhere else, even though their love light for you still burned and your love for them was bright.''

Now you might need to go on, ''Your mom is going to marry Ted. He will be living in your house and doing some of the things for you that your dad used to do when he and your mom were still married. In time you may get used to having Ted help you with things. You may get close to him and he may get close to you. [Light a new candle representing the stepparent.] When that happens, there will be one more person for you to love and who loves you. The important thing for you to remember is that the light of love you feel for your dad will not go out. Loving is not like soup that you dish up until it is all gone. You can love as many people as you get close to. But no one will make you blow out any of your candles. You do not have to take the love you feel for your dad away to love Ted.'' With whatever variation fits, you need to give the child permission to grow close to a new caretaker.

This ritual is easily adapted to almost all circumstances where a child feels that he must extinguish his feelings for one important adult in order to please another. Even very young children have been known to object, rightfully, ''You're trying to make me blow out my candle,'' when they are caught in a tug-of-war between different caretakers. If the child was not as well nurtured in early life as in the example we used above, that language, too, can be modified to fit the circumstances.

Because the candle was chosen for its symbolic connection with how children perceive love, as light and warmth, it is important to close the ritual carefully. ''I can see, John, that you understand about loving. I don't think you need the candles any more today to help you. This candle is not really your mother. She will not stop loving you if we put it out. Are you ready to help me blow it out?'' This needs to be repeated for each candle before it is extinguished.

If you are the primary caretaker for a child who has suffered a loss, allow as much continuity as possible in the child's daily routine. Even week-old infants seem to be disquieted by a change in their daily schedules; and with older children, too, it is wise to communicate that things have not changed completely. You might be very specific in explaining these things to the child: "You and Mommy used to read a story every night before you went to bed. Now she is gone and I will read to you at night."

If possible, try to avoid subsequent losses immediately after a major loss. Postpone the change to a new school or church, the cutting of ties with friends or grandparents. In divorce especially, children are apt to suffer such additional losses. Even the daily routine is disrupted, if a nonworking parent must take a job; and the standard of living may be altered for the worse.

Whatever the reason for separation, care must be taken in arranging visits between the noncustodial parent and the child. It is not easy to watch someone else parent your child, and a visiting parent sometimes will back out of an appointment at the last minute. Or the change in plan may occur because of some unexpected event; such things happen more frequently because the parent and child are leading separate lives. In either case, it is most important to contact your child directly to explain why you are not able to make the promised visit, and to reschedule it for another time.

Sometimes the visiting arrangements that have been set up at the start of the separation prove to be unmanageable. Jim's foster parents find him upset and unhappy following visits by his birth mother. They feel it is harmful for him to see her, and it disrupts the rest of their family. They insist—against the social worker's judgment of what is best for Jim—that the visits be less frequent. Suzanne's father has been falling behind in his child support payments. Her mother is thinking about stopping their visits until he catches up. These families should bear in mind that any such reduction of visits to the child constitutes an additional loss—the loss of what was promised, what the child has counted on. All the concerns in helping the child with the original loss are just as important here; the child must be able to understand the change and to express his feelings about it.

Children often become oversensitive or react with unusual intensity to injuries, or imagined injuries, in the period that follows a loss. They feel particularly vulnerable, and this feeling is often reinforced by the remaining parent, who may show his own anxiety and need for support by frequent visits to the doctor or teacher. Bumps and scratches that were once quickly forgotten will acquire unusual importance and need solicitous care. If they are briefly separated from the caretaker, or the caretaker becomes ill, they may to imagine that this person too will be taken from them or will decide not to return.

There are two ways to deal with a child's heightened feeling of vulnerability. First, you should make clear to him that you will look out for him, and that you respect his fears (even if they seem unreasonable to you). Second, encourage the child to ask for what he needs: "I need an extra hug," or the like. If the needs are overwhelming to you, try to give what is asked for at least the first time, and then bargain for a change that is more acceptable. Obviously, there will be some requests that cannot be met: to bring back the absent family member, to stay home from work. But many things can be worked out to make the child feel more peaceful: "I can't be Mommy but I can cuddle with you." "I have to go to work now but we can have extra time together when I come home."

What Should I Do First?

Sometimes when we are responsible for helping a child with the initial impact of a loss we feel anxious about where to begin. It seems as if there is so much to remember. But it doesn't really matter where you start, or if you remember everything the first or second or third time. Often the child will lead the way, showing you what is needed and when by the questions that he asks. Then you can confidently follow his cues, knowing you are doing just what needs to be done. If this doesn't happen, follow your own instincts, taking things up when they seem appropriate to you. The important thing is that you are concerned about doing your best to help the child, and that you establish an atmosphere of respect for the child's needs. In such a climate of continuing trust, where you are willing to address his questions and concerns honestly, the child will be able to get on with the work of grieving that must follow.

2.
Early Reactions
to Separation and Loss

EVERY PERSON'S EXPERIENCE WITH GRIEF will be his own, of course. People's mourning responses, though, do fall into three basic phases: early grief, acute grief, and subsiding grief. Though there may be overlapping, skipping around, or returns to previous stages, each phase has a number of components that follow in a somewhat predictable order.

No matter how trivial a loss might seem, the same process must be gone through each time, though the length and intensity of the experience will differ. It may take years to recover from a major loss. But the symptoms of grief and recovery can also be fully experienced in as little as ten seconds, as is pointed out vividly in this example from *How to Survive the Loss of a Love*:

> We run to a ringing phone and just as we pick it up, the caller hangs up. Our first thought might be, "Oh, no. I couldn't have missed it" (shock/denial). Our next thought, "Why didn't they hold on a little longer?" or "Why didn't I get here sooner?" (anger, which can be expressed against

the other person, ourselves, or more often both). Then: "Gee, I really wanted to talk with somebody" (depression). And finally: "Oh, well, if it was important they'll call back" (understanding, acceptance), and we return to what we were doing, or call another friend, or buy an answering machine, depending on how we individually deal with the aftermath of loss. The whole process might take place in a few seconds, but the three stages of recovery have been experienced, the body has healed, and we are ready to continue with life (Colgrove et al., p. 16).

PHASE ONE: EARLY GRIEF

The first phase, early grief, manifests itself in three ways: shock and numbing, alarm, and denial. Let's look at how each of these reactions can be recognized and then talk about what you might do to help a child cope with the stresses involved.

Shock and Numbing

Ellie is usually a busy toddler, constantly exploring her environment, eager to engage in shared play such as peek-a-boo. Last week her mother was hospitalized for emergency surgery. Her father has been stopping by the hospital on his way to and from work, so he is less available to his daughter than he usually is. The babysitter, whom Ellie does not know well, reports concern that something is the matter with Ellie. She seems withdrawn, sitting with a sad, glazed expression on her face. It is hard to draw her into play, and then her play seems almost mechanical. What happened to that busy, happy runabout?

Once the realization of a loss or separation has begun, many children begin to go through the motions of their daily life mechanically, like robots. They may seem lifeless, automatically smiling on cue. Underlying this behavior there is usually a good deal of apprehension, and their "flatness" may be broken by outbursts of panic. It is not unusual for children to become very withdrawn, ignoring their normal activities and sitting for long periods gazing into space. This is most striking in a child Ellie's age, who is normally constantly on the go.

You may worry that the news you bring of a loss or separation will cause your child to break down or come apart. But you can be reassured. In times of great stress we shut down our awareness emotionally, sometimes intellectually, and occasionally physically. If you have ever had a severe accident you may have experienced that in the beginning there was surprisingly little pain. Such is the common reaction to the news of a separation or loss. A built-in mechanism operates to screen out devastating information and to prevent us from becoming overloaded. Certainly strong reactions are likely, but chances are they will be overshadowed or delayed by these internal screening responses.

The first reaction is numbness, or sometimes acute panic followed by numbness. There may be a sense of watching the event as if it were happening to someone else. This lack of sensation may last a few hours to a week. It alternates with outbursts of extremely intense distress or anger or bothas the reality of the loss begins to register, leading to intense pining, heightened irritability, and sobbing or crying out loud for the lost person.

When you first tell a child about a loss, even if you are careful to use words that he can understand, he may react casually. Then he may cry later, at bedtime, and need to be told again. This may dismay and confuse you as you try to figure out what the child actually heard, and whether he is truly untouched by the information.

If there is forewarning of an impending loss, the trauma can be made less severe. Telling the child ahead of time lets him play and replay the separation experience to come, learning and practicing his coping skills before he must call them into action. In this case he is less likely to be overcome and thrown into a state of shock by the event.

Even when they are prepared for an impending change, however, many children hang onto their initial denial and disbelief. They will not accept that the loss will happen; or they count on something magical to prevent it—the parents will change their minds, the dying person will get better. It is not unusual for a child to believe the news only when the separation has actually occurred, and even then the child may cling to her belief that the separation will be short-lived.

Alarm

Because children look to their parents to keep them safe, the loss of a family member heightens their sense of vulnerability. Their protector is either gone or has proven unable to maintain the children's safety. In families where one child dies, it is quite common for the other children, though previously well adjusted, to become very reluctant and anxious about going to school, to be depressed, and to feel severe separation anxiety.

Part of the shock of separation and loss is physical—the alarm caused by the sudden realization of danger to oneself. This arouses bodily reactions that exist to help us defend ourselves from danger by running, fighting, or immobilization. These include increased heart rate and muscular tension, sweating, dryness of mouth, and bowel and bladder relaxation. Shortness of breath is common, as well as deep sighing and rapid breathing, especially when talking about the lost person. These reactions come in waves lasting from minutes to hours, and may culminate in a general sense of weakness and exhaustion, as if it were too much effort to go on.

Some psychologists believe that the insomnia so common during the first year after a major loss is an outgrowth of this alertness to danger. When your trust in the world as a benign place is shaken, it is difficult to let down your guard and sleep.

Because of this built-up stress and these changes in bodily functioning, those who have suffered a recent loss may be increasingly prone to infection. The child may have one cold, ear infection, or gastrointestinal upset after another. Noses run constantly. Skin rashes, heightened allergic responses, bleeding of the gums, and bronchial inflammation are frequent. Children may pick at themselves, biting their nails or cuticles, twiddling their hair and sometimes even pulling it out.

These symptoms of stress may appear within the first forty-eight hours following news of a separation or loss; they may occur as the child begins to believe that the loss or change is to be permanent or long-lasting; or they may accompany significant anniversaries, holidays, a remarriage that makes the original parental reunion impossible, or an impending adoption finalization that makes the severance from the first family irreversible.

How can you help? It is useless for you to tell the child, "Don't worry." She is unable to control her responses. But there are things that you can do to help a child in this phase of grieving. Most of them involve common sense.

As we have discussed, it is imperative that the child be told who will take care of her, and that she be helped to believe that this caretaker knows how to care for her, wants to, and has her best interests and safety at heart. Many children take physical comfort and sense your concern when you give them special foods, particularly ones they are used to eating when ill. Soft foods such as applesauce and mashed potato, and warm, milky substances are often a reassuring reminder of early, easier times.

The folk wisdom that we use when we bring home a new puppy can be helpful in these situations. The young pup that you bring home will be frightened and lonely at first, and you are prepared to accept that he will whine and have trouble sleeping. You do not take this as a rejection of the comforts of your family, but rather as an outgrowth of his separation. Children respond in similar ways, and their caretakers should refrain from feeling slighted when such things happen.

With a new puppy we try to make the transition as easy as possible. We wrap up a hot water bottle or a jug of hot water in an old towel for the puppy to snuggle with. Children who have suffered a recent loss also respond well to snuggling against a warm, soft, rough surface. Many of them are better able to face

the dark, lonely, scary time of bedtime if they are tucked in between flannel sheets, or if the cold top sheet is removed and they
can sleep with the blanket directly against them. Like newborns,
they may feel more comfortable when tucked in tightly, or even
when wrapped up in a flannel blanket and then tucked in.
During the day some children want to wear extra layers of
clothing, to reduce their coldness and shock and to help them
feel lovingly wrapped and armored against possible harm.

With a new puppy we often provide a ticking alarm clock to
allay the silence and loneliness of the night or to cover up strange
noises. Children who have suffered a recent loss may have less
difficulty settling down for bed if they are allowed to drift off to
sleep with a radio playing softly, or if they are put to bed where
they can overhear the reassuring sounds of grownups talking or
the television going. (Obviously the wisdom of the latter is
determined by whether the adult conversation or television is
comforting rather than scary in tone.)

Unfortunately, a child's anxieties may be much slower than
a new puppy's to disappear. Past experiences have proved to the
child that he cannot count on adults to provide safety. The world
seems an unreliable, unsafe place. Fear of the dark is common
and may last for years. The child may fear sirens. He may have
recurrent dreams, either based on past realities or symbolically
related to the loss. He may be prone to nightmares or night terrors, in which he cries out with open eyes, seemingly aware but
unable to remember the event the next morning. About one-fifth
of the grieving children Bowlby reports on showed intense separation anxieties and experienced acute night terrors; about one-
fourth clung excessively during the day or insisted on sleeping
with a parent or sibling at night. Between one-fourth and one-
third were overactive and aggressive. Some engaged in unpro-
voked violence toward peers or adults and destroyed property
(Bowlby III, p. 316).

The best treatment for this long-term anxiety is to provide
the child with a trusted, lifetime caretaker who will share the
child's fears, comfort him, and sustain him. Remember, too, that

what might otherwise be normal separation experiences will take on extra significance to the child in this stage of grief. George is still having trouble being left with a sitter or at his day care center following his parents' separation. He cries and begs; and often his mother must tear herself away, feeling guilty over his obvious distress. Now he has begun to tremble when they park the car outside the center, even before they are inside. His mother has to go to work. What can she do?

One way to help such a child is to be reliable about returning at the expected time. Another is to help the child focus on the day's routine so that he can predict when to expect her. George's mother might say, "After lunch you have your nap time. Then there is circle and play time, then time on the swings and in the sandbox. Then Mommy comes." If the child is old enough to tell time you might want to invest in a watch, or help the child find another way to keep track of the passage of time. If you are to be delayed, it is best to call the child and personally explain what has happened. Some children, particularly young ones, feel safer if the parent leaves something the child knows is important—the house key, for example—behind with the child. With this talisman in his keeping, he is more sure that the parent will not disappear for good. It is also important to reassure the child that you are not leaving him because you are angry, or because he has been angry or sad; that you will return; and that you will be thinking about him while you are apart.

Denial and Disbelief

Tonja, age 8, has recently attended the funeral services for her grandmother, who has lived with her since she was an infant. Tonight as she is setting the table there is a knock at the door. Tonja runs to answer it, exclaiming, "There, that's Grammy! I'll let her in."

Eleven-year-old Ray seems to be weathering the first few weeks of his parents' separation quite well. But as he comes home from playing at a friend's he hurries in the door calling, "Dad, Dad?" His mother reminds him, "Daddy doesn't live here any more, Ray, you know that." "I thought I saw him driving down the street and I thought maybe he was coming home," Ray says.

In the most easily recognized form of denial there is obviously an element of disbelief. The child just doesn't accept that the loss will happen or has happened. Or the loss is "forgotten"—the child expects to hear the voice on the phone, or sees and hears things that make her turn around expectantly, or runs toward a distant person calling the name of the absent family member. Just as bereaved adults often sense the presence of their loved one sitting in a favorite chair, or think they hear the person speaking, children have these experiences too; and sometimes when they report them we fear they have been hallucinating. Both in daydreams and in night dreams, the child senses the presence of the lost person so convincingly that it seems impossible the person is really away.

The child may refuse to hear the news of a separation or loss, covering her ears and saying, "No, no!" Psychologists tell us that denial is a conscious or unconscious defense that all of us use to avoid, reduce, or prevent anxiety when we are threatened. We use it to shut out of our awareness things that would be too disturbing to know. Denial is the earliest defense to emerge in our psychological development. Even infants use it, closing their eyes and turning their heads away as if to say, "If I can't see it, it isn't happening."

Some children refuse to believe that the parent is no longer available. They cherish memories, mementos, letters, pictures. They beg to see the parent, to call. When the absent parent is dead or when the caretaking parent feels great resentment or competition toward the other parent, this can be problematical. But difficult as these behaviors may be for the adult, they are a healthy sign in the child. They demonstrate that this child is able to form strong, close attachments to caretakers, to accept nurturing, to love.

Other children, just as strongly attached, will reject the absent parent who they feel has rejected them. Sometimes the child will go so far as to deny that the absent parent exists or ever existed. The child may also defend herself against the pain of loss by denying the importance of the person who is gone. "Joanie, it looks like we need to find another family for you," her worker says. "So?" says Joanie sullenly. Deprecation, contempt, and other such devaluation of the lost person are all forms of denial used by the grieving child.

Sometimes this denial or deprecation will be encouraged or even demanded by the caretaking adult. The child receives clear but often covert messages that in order to please he must act as if nothing bad has happened, or that he must deny his feelings and pretend to be pleased or grateful for the change. "I really didn't like it there, I'd rather be here," children may say to comply with these messages. Much literature refers to the "honeymoon period," that time following relocation from one family to another or from family to institution when the child is no trouble, fits in easily, is eager to please. Many times this "see how good I am" phase grows out of the attempt to please the caretaking parent as well as to demonstrate magically to the absent parent that the child will do anything, even be good, if only the parent will return and reclaim him.

Denial can also involve belief that the loss is real but exclude the feelings that rightfully go with such a loss. In children there is often some magical thinking involved in this phenomenon: "This can't really be happening, because if it were I would feel bad, and I don't so it's not really happening." It can also arise, as we have seen, from a desire to please the current caretaker; they may parrot, "It's really all for the best; they couldn't take care of me anyway."

Other children are in a similar situation to the adult who cannot afford to let down emotional defenses because of real responsibilities—children, a job, getting resettled. Like the adult, they may have to master new social and academic environments, perhaps including integration into a new family; and they isolate their feelings, saving their energies to master these life adjustments.

Occasionally, children avoid and deny their feelings at some time in the process of grieving as a way of allowing a time-out or reprieve from the pain and work of mourning.

You do not need to be unduly concerned about denial or avoidance of feelings unless it continues for longer than three to six months without interruption. If this happens, the child is more likely to remain stuck in the preliminary stages of grief, which often leads to potentially serious difficulties in forming other relationships, eventual feelings of emptiness, and trouble getting over the trauma of loss and on with life.

Hyperactivity as Denial

Paula, always a verbal child, has seemed to talk or just make noise with her mouth ever since she has come into the Johnson household. It is hard for anyone else to complete a thought or a conversation because of her racket. When she isn't chattering she is fidgeting. She squirms and giggles and bumps things and bangs. It is hard to relax with her around because of the constant stimulation. Mealtimes are a zoo.

Like Paula, the child you know might show symptoms of denial after a separation or loss by physically acting out mental avoidance. By keeping very busy, the child can avoid thinking about what has happened. As reminders make it harder to keep reality at bay the child becomes more and more frenzied; there is constant activity or conversation, and sometimes increased masturbation both publicly and privately. It becomes difficult to get the child to go to bed and stay there, where the quiet dark will invite thoughts and feelings about the loss.

Children who are working at denial in this way may also have difficulty being alone. They need constant playmates, company, or diversion to help keep their minds off what has happened. Adolescents use headphones or the telephone to fill their quiet times and block their own internal voices, or they use alcohol or drugs to help them forget or stop caring about the loss.

PHASE TWO: ACUTE GRIEF

The second phase of mourning, acute grief, has several stages: yearning and pining, searching, strong feeling, disorganization, despair, and finally reorganization. Looking at each of them in turn may help in understanding the part they play in working through grief.

Yearning and Pining

Cindy's mother died two years ago, when Cindy was six. Since her mother's death Cindy has found her life very difficult; her father is remote and demanding, and she spends a lot of time dreaming that things could be the way they used to be. One Sunday afternoon she goes with a friend to see Walt Disney's *Snow White*. "I'm wishing, I'm wishing," sings the heroine, and tears roll down Cindy's cheeks. Snow White is just like her, she thinks: people are always asking her to work hard, and no one notices her. She is left in a dark forest, scared and alone. When will a prince come to wake her from her glass coffin and take her away to be happy forever?

When we suffer a loss or separation there is a deep core within us, sometimes felt physically, that wishes for a different ending. This is not what is supposed to happen, we think; this is not how things are supposed to work out. Hope flickers over and over that somehow things will return to the way they were, that the lost loved one will return. In the continuum between anxiety and despair our feelings keep going back and forth, moved by this recurring hope. Cindy will think of Snow White's story for years to come whenever she feels especially lonely or her life seems hard and unfair; she holds on to its happy ending, keeping her hope alive.

Like Cindy, a great many children identify with those they see in books, television shows, movies, and real life who suffer a loss and later experience reunion. The stories of Snow White, Cinderella, and Lassie; movies and plays such as *The Wizard of Oz, Annie, Oliver*; and tales such as those in *Little House on the*

Prairie, with its recurring loss/restitution themes, all become favorites. It may be bad now, these stories say, but it will be fixed by and by. This yearning and pining is common in all of us; when things do work out in the story, we are moved to tears by the restitution—and our tears carry both joy for the fictional character and perhaps pain for our own hidden yearning.

This stage of grief will recur throughout life, in our wishes that a parent long dead could be there to see some accomplishment, new baby, or marriage; or in the wish that a parental relationship could be a closer one, even after we have accepted its imperfections.

Children find this task in the grieving process recycled by visits from the separated parent. If the visits prove unreliable, the child's caretaker may decide that the pain of yearning is too hard on the child. From what we know, however, this part of grieving is best resolved over the long term by experiencing the yearning, by being able to share it without it being discounted, and by letting go a bit at a time of the hope that the wish will come true. Visiting also allows the child, through trial and error, to work towards not only accepting the situation but making the best of it. It helps him take as completely as possible the good available from the visiting parent, without losing her completely; and it helps remove the child's feelings that the vanished parent found him unlovable or not good enough. Through repeatedly being frustrated and letting go, the child gradually understands the reality of the separation.

This conflict between the need to relinquish what has been lost and the wish to hold onto it—the pull between the past and the future—is the keynote to grief. Normal grieving is the process of working through the ambivalence by identifying conflicting impulses, suffering through one's awareness, and eventually mastering the feelings. Simos discusses how this ambivalence of grieving may take many forms:

> The bereaved show both a desire to be alone and a craving for companionship. There is an attempt to avoid reminders of the past, yet a compulsion or urgency to talk and dwell on

the loss exists. There is a conflict between being passive and active, dependent and independent, regressive and moving forward, and between being supersensitive to the least slight from others and rebuffing overtures of help and sympathy when offered. The conflict shows in the insistence that life has lost all meaning coupled with the simultaneous competent attention to the daily routines of living. The bereaved alternate between despair and hope, between anger at the deceased and guilt at failing to keep him alive. They are torn between wanting to be helpless and to be exploitive of others and the fear that they will lose all their friends if they are. They may compulsively seek distractions only to discover they have no interest in these very distractions. They may be curious about some aspect of the loss and at the same time not wish to know the answer (Simos, p. 55).

These conflicts are amplified if there is a high ratio of hate to love in the relationship with the lost person.

These conflicting pulls are exhausting. Many bereaved children and adults require more sleep than usual and still wake without feeling rested. Parents of children who have suffered a separation or loss are wise to plan for earlier bedtimes and perhaps a quiet time in the afternoon, and to help the child alternate activity with passive occupations like soaking in a warm tub, listening to music, or watching fish in an aquarium.

Regression is a common companion to the conflict and fatigue that results from the yearning and pining stage. Terry, who is six, has reverted to whining like a preschooler. It drives his mother crazy. She needs to know that many children temporarily give up a skill they had mastered earlier in their development at times like this, returning to the behavior of an earlier age. This is seen not only during the stress of loss and separation, but also during other life changes. The toddler may begin wetting or wanting a bottle following the birth of a sibling; the busy, independent school-age youngster may seek the comfort of a lap when things are hard.

Such regression, even to a much earlier form of behavior, is normal; adults need not resist or worry about it. If children are allowed to return to familiar, simpler ground until their equilibrium is restored, their energies renewed, and their courage mobilized, they often will emerge stronger and more competent than before. And a child's need to regress in one area does not mean he will regress in all areas. Parents who are seriously troubled by their child's babyish behavior might request that he restrict it to the privacy of home, as long as they also clearly give him permission to feel and act in those ways when he needs special care. If you find such behavior too disquieting, short-term play therapy may provide an arena for healing through temporary regression.

Finally, though some elements of yearning and pining are always present, a loss or separation may also involve an element of relief. This happens when the loss is experienced as better than the state that preceded it. The slow and wasting death of a loved one, the separation from an alcoholic or abusive parent, the divorce where peace replaces the fighting—all are heart-breaking separations that can be followed by relief.

The child who never becomes aware of his conflicting needs to hold on to what was and to let go, or who is not able to admit these needs to himself or to others, may avoid the pain that follows. But the conflict that is buried is never resolved. It may carry itself into other areas of his life, making it difficult to begin anew, or it may fester, breaking forth later in life when more losses or yearnings are experienced.

Searching

When Dan was nine he was separated from his parents by court intervention. Lately he has been taking the bus to his old neighborhood, though he knows his parents have moved long ago and their whereabouts are unknown. He likes to stand outside their apartment building, not doing much. He would laugh if he were accused of looking for his parents; but still he is drawn back time and again, feeling that if he could just talk to them now, they could work things out.

Searching seems often to be an outgrowth of yearning and pining, especially when a child identifies with a fictional character who took action and found a happy ending. This stage includes several elements:

1. Preoccupied and intense thought about the lost person, involving a compulsion to speak of him, to review a lifetime of memories about him, and to ignore anything not relevant to his presence.
2. A sense of waiting for something to happen and a direction of attention to places where the person is likely to be found.
3. Restless, sometimes aimless moving around with an inability to sit still, a constant searching for something to do, a scanning of the environment. This is not unlike the agitated behavior described under denial, and has a similar outcome for many children, who are medicated for hyperactivity when their behavior is in fact a normal reaction to loss.

To the observer these behaviors may appear compulsive and irrational. It is easier to understand them, though, if we think of our own searching impulses in reaction to benign losses —the tongue that explores the place where a tooth has come out, or the searching and re-searching in the same place for a misplaced item that we know was there not long ago.

This drive to retrieve is particularly understandable if the lost loved one is not dead, but lives away from us. In these cases, such as divorce, foster care, and adoption, the search serves to test reality. Each effort brings the hope of remaking the past, whether it makes possible the changes necessary for reunion or whether it breaks the fantasy of reunion, reaffirming the inevitability and permanence of the loss.

There appear to be biological precursors that influence this behavior. Our behavior towards loved ones, Bowlby tells us, encourages the continuation of our bonds to them; and any situation that seems to endanger those bonds will elicit instinctive actions to prevent a loss. Every separation, however brief, may cause an immediate, automatic, and strong effort both to recover the family, especially the member to whom attachment is closest, and to discourage that member from going away again. Our standard response to the loss of a loved one is first to recover him and then to scold him. Parents who have spent frantic hours trying to find the child who is late coming home from school, and then have greeted the returning child with an angry outburst, understand this well.

This ingrained behavior causes problems, though. Our urges to recover and scold are automatic responses to any and every loss, whether what is lost is really retrievable or not. The bereaved child commonly experiences a compelling urge to recover the lost loved one even when she knows the attempt is hopeless. Moreover, says Bowlby, "when the effort to restore the bond is not successful sooner or later the effort wanes. But usually it does not cease. On the contrary, evidence shows that, at perhaps increasingly long intervals, the effort to restore the bond is renewed; the pangs of grief and perhaps an urge to search are then experienced afresh. This means that the person's attachment behavior is remaining constantly primed and that, in conditions still to be defined, it becomes activated anew." (Bowlby III, p. 42)

This phase draws to a close only when enough searching has taken place that the child accepts that she has mustered every effort available. Even then a conscious or unconscious contract may be made—a "bargain" where the child acknowledges her helplessness to attain part of the goal without the intervention of a more powerful other—parent or deity. The child may promise to "always be good," or to "wait forever," or some variation on these. This fits snugly into children's normal magical thinking, and it is reinforced by fairy and folk tales—in order to get what you want you must strive diligently long enough or wait patiently long enough, and then the powers that be grant your wish.

Internal bargains such as these are seen in adolescents and adults as well. One part of the awareness accepts that the loss is permanent, while the other, with only marginal accessibility to conscious thought, believes that the person can somehow be recovered in this world or the next. Bowlby gives an example of a fifteen-year-old girl whose mother died suddenly of a cerebral hemorrhage. Before the death, the girl's weight had caused disagreement between the two; the mother felt that the girl should diet and lose weight. During the period before the young woman's seventeenth birthday she dieted diligently and became quite slim. On the eve of her birthday she was euphoric and dreamy. She took a long walk. But by the end of the following day she had begun an eating binge that lasted for many weeks. "Having conformed with her mother's wishes over the dieting, it appeared she had been expecting her mother to return on her birthday; it was a bargain which had not been kept." (Bowlby III, p. 372)

Those who wish to help a child with the grief process can expect signs of disbelief, manifested in searching and dreaming behavior, even after reason dictates that such behavior is futile. So long as the child believes that the loss is yet retrievable, he is impelled to action. Divorcing parents, for example, often shake their heads and recount how when they met to discuss division of property and financial settlements their youngster put on soft music and turned down the lights, to help them get back together again.

The helping adult should be patient with these behaviors, knowing that they are part of coming to accept the change. Impatience with the child who is preoccupied with searching can delay rather than facilitate grief work. Curt remarks urging the child not to dwell on the past only cut off the sharing and make the bereaved child feel misunderstood. Through repeated attempts at recovery and repeated disappointments, the child will slowly and painfully relinquish his searching behavior. If denied the chance to do this, huge and fruitless amounts of his emotional energies remain tied to the lost or separated loved one, and the ability to use these energies in other areas of living is impeded.

Strong Feelings: Sadness, Anger, Guilt, and Shame

Brian has been very upset about his parents' separation. His mother, trying to talk to him about it, tells him that both his parents are concerned about him. "Oh sure!" Brian yells, jumping up from his chair and knocking it over. "You don't care at all! I hate you, I hate you, you and Daddy too." Sobbing, he runs to his room and slams the door.

Much of the outcome of a child's loss or separation experience hinges on how adults allow and even encourage the child to accept his strong feelings about what has happened. The helping adult must understand that the recovery to creative, healthy living involves pain. There is no short cut. The adult should be available to the hurting child, give the child as much time with these feelings as he needs, and avoid messages that tell the child what he should and should not be feeling.

The person best qualified to help does not separate feelings into "good feelings" and "bad feelings," but rather understands that we feel as we feel. Feelings vary from person to person, and these variations are out of conscious control. They cannot be changed by scoldings, criticism, and disapproval, nor can we tell ourselves how to feel. A feeling is just a bodily signal of an emotional state—our response to something that has touched us, like the itch that follows a mosquito bite. To say to a child, "Don't be sad" is useless, like saying, "Don't itch." We complicate grief work when we send a child messages to hurry it up, such as "don't take it so hard," "pull yourself together," "crying does no good."

Brian's mother will need to face her child's onslaught of intense feeling without drawing back, flinching, or offering reassurances in order to turn off the outpouring. Brian must be treated with empathy and respect—not pity, or panic, or attempts to structure the grief process in a way that speeds it up or tones it down.

Grieving adults and children share the problem that those around them misunderstand how best to help them. Our society emphasizes competence, strength, and accomplishment—and normal grief work involves opposite qualities. "Because normal behavior in grief is so different from what is considered normal behavior generally," Simos comments, "it is not surprising to find that the grieving person does not know whether his behavior is normal or pathological. Family and friends are often of little help because they too are confused over this issue" (Simos, p. 99).

Helping adults, as Bowlby points out, may avoid sympathizing with such feelings and encouraging their expression, especially if any display of sympathy seems to lead to prolonged crying, periods of irritability and dissatisfaction, or angry outbursts. "Looking after a grieving child," he says, "is exacting and unrewarding work. . . . After a small child has lost a parent, therefore, it is by no means unusual for him to be subjected to strong pressure to "forget" his grief and, instead, to become interested in whatever his current caregiver thinks may distract him" (Bowlby, p. 397). When this happens, the child is at a much greater disadvantage than the adult who finds his expressions of feeling discounted. Should immediate family prove unhelpful, the child has fewer avenues to follow in finding sympathetic persons who will allow her feelings.

Even the supportive adult who tries to help a child in this stage of grief may face anger and hostility, however. Nothing but the return of the lost person will bring true comfort, and efforts that fall short of return are seen as useless. The helper who seems to want the child to accept the loss may be as keenly resented as if he had caused the loss, and his efforts to help may be met with extreme anger and blame. This is not the time, though, for the helper to defend himself against accusations, or to argue with the child about them. The adult can be most helpful if he understands why the child makes him a target for anger. It helps to have some experience, as most counselors do, with being at once an object of hostility and a source of emotional support.

Be prepared for grief, including this stage of strong feelings, to take a long time to abate. It would be difficult to over-emphasize the long duration of grief with its intense distress and disablement, or to overstate the damage that results from trying to shorten the process. Once the stage of intense feeling has begun, it usually takes between six and twelve weeks for the worst of the pain to diminish, and it often takes two or more years before the grief process is completed. Children need at least as much time to come to grips with their losses as adults do.

In this day of fast food and instant gratification, most children have had little experience with learning patience. Let the child know that it will take a long time before he feels better —the greater the loss, the longer the time. Don't rush to get him into a "more productive" emotional state, or minimize the extent to which he can feel the loss. And reassure him that not only will the healing happen, but it is going on even in his hurting, for hurting is part of the cure.

We will deal at length in later chapters with the complications that occur if the child's feelings are not permitted, encouraged, and supported during this stage of grief. For the adult who is willing to provide permission, encouragement, and support, here are some suggestions.

1. When the child shares her sadness, anger, guilt, or shame through verbal or physical expression, don't ask her to postpone, deny, or cover up her feelings. Grief that is postponed can return months or even years later to haunt the child.

2. Feelings take precedence over almost everything else except physical safety. This means that when the child tries to share her feelings the adult ends the phone conversation with another, turns off the cooking pot, or puts down the newspaper, and thereby communicates, "Your feelings are important and I will find time to listen to them. You are not bothering me."

3. The helping adult can share his own strength with the child by getting physically close to her when she experiences strong feelings. What you say may not be as important as what you do—the support of a hand on the knee, an arm around the shoulder, a lap to sit on, or a shoulder to cry against can reassure

the child. Often it helps just to sit there with the child while she cries or rants.

4. Even if the child's feelings about the loss are different from your own, they are not to be denied. Do not tell the child what to feel, or for how long.

5. Include the child in family mourning so he can share in loving support and a sense of communal pain.

6. Do not criticize or seem shocked by the child's statements and feelings. Criticism can add another layer to feelings, delaying the healing of the original feeling. It is the recognition, acceptance, and validation of each emotion as it occurs that lets the child move from one emotional state to another so that grief can be completed.

Disorganization

Molly seems to be over the major emotional reaction to her mother's remarriage. She cries less and less, and her irritability and angry outbursts are tapering off. "We've weathered it," her mother says to herself, with a sigh of relief. And then Molly's teacher requests a conference. Formerly a good student, Molly is falling behind in school. She doesn't seem to be able to settle down and begin her work; and during class discussion it is as if she is on another planet. She rarely knows the place to begin reading when she is called on, and she has trouble finishing her work. What can be the matter?

Grieving is extremely demanding work. It takes so much energy that little is left to attend to other aspects of living. It is quite normal for previously competent, active people to find themselves sitting around aimlessly, their minds drifting off to thoughts of the loss. It becomes difficult, even impossible, to concentrate on a task and to complete it without error. Simple decisions are exhausting, and to begin a new project or to organize one's day seems a monumental challenge. Adults in this frame of mind frequently feel angry with themselves, wondering if they are losing their minds or falling apart.

This typical grieving reaction poses difficulties both for the bereaved child and for the adults around her. School, obviously, can become a major difficulty; like Molly, many children are unable to concentrate, learn, and retain information. Their performance may drop to the point that they need to repeat a grade. Reading—especially in social studies, where facts must be pulled into a cohesive whole, or in English, where themes must be explored in depth—poses great difficulty. In addition, there seems to be an interesting symbolic reaction to arithmetic: problems that involve subtracting or dividing may set off the child's internal reactions to personal loss. It is not at all unusual for a grieving child to be able to add and multiply but to "forget" the same numerical facts when applied to division and subtraction.

Many teachers will give some leeway to the child who is undergoing a major separation or loss. Too frequently, though, they underestimate the longevity of the stage of disorganization, which usually lasts well past the first anniversary of the loss; symptoms of disorganization often come and go through the second year. A study conducted in the Arlington, Massachusetts public schools with forty-nine bereaved elementary school children found that nearly all of them showed a decline in grades. The children became passive and withdrawn from relationships in general. With good support from the home, one-third of the group recovered from their trauma at the end of the first year—but two-thirds were still set back and working on resolving their grief issues (Grollman 1975, p. 164).

It does children like Molly little good to be told to try harder, or to be labeled lazy or daydreamers. Instead, you might try to figure out how you call your own wandering attention back to a task. What internal steps and words do you use? Some children will be helped by a discussion that gives concrete advice.

Ten-year-old Roger, for example, was still showing lack of concentration and scattered thought patterns well into the third year after his move into a foster home. As a result he was doing poorly in school, though he was enthusiastic about playing basketball in gym class and he was an avid football fan. We talked about how athletes focused themselves by thinking through the plays before a game, getting themselves mentally "up" for the competition. Roger's foster mother agreed to be his "coach," and gave him a pep talk each morning: "Okay, you can do it. You can beat that old math. Go to it!" Roger helped himself by imagining how the players began together in a circle; he decided to try his basketball handclap and a "Let's go!" as he sat down to his math. He made a mental picture of himself cheering himself on. When he found his mind wandering, he clapped his hands together quietly to bring himself back to his task. Although these methods did not hasten his grief process, they did allow him to keep his mind enough on his schoolwork that he no longer forfeited his recesses.

This kind of concrete suggestion, drawn from a child's interests and experiences, can be as creative as the adult can make it. It can be adapted to other hobbies, interests, talents, and play themes. It would be a mistake, however, to expect the child to use it constantly throughout the school day, for such exercises are tiring and the child may not have enough energy to continue them. If the technique is applied to one problem at a time, the youngster will have the chance to feel successful and in charge.

Time should be allowed for physical play, as well. Children may show little zest for normal pleasures because of their painful grief, and they will often play less well. But they need time to return to life's pleasures as well as its responsibilities. It is important, then, in helping the child who is falling behind in school, to avoid cutting heavily into time for play and social interactions with other children.

Children who have a set time to talk about their loss with a parent or another helping person are more likely to be able to focus themselves on schoolwork. A school counselor or psychologist can be really supportive here, by providing a place at school where it is all right to think about the loss, instead of always having to attend to class responsibilities. This helps the child see school as an understanding rather than a hostile environment.

The grieving child often has trouble following directions during this stage; and this can cause problems at home as well as at school. Sent to get three items in the living room, a child might return with just one, or call, "What was I supposed to get?" Deep in thought, he might not hear a request until it has been repeated a number of times—and then wonder why his parents are "always yelling at me." Daily responsibilities like washing or brushing teeth, no matter how routine, may be forgotten. A parent's exasperation is understandable, but it is best to calmly suggest ways that the child can help himself remember his responsibilities. "John, look at me. I want you to go into the living room and [holding up one finger] pick up your jacket, [holding up a second finger] pick up your socks, and [holding up a third finger] pick up your comic books. Now tell me, what are you going to do?" Going over items with the child this way helps; he can show that he has heard, and then singsong to himself, "jacket, socks, books," or remember the image of the three fingers: "Now let's see, there was something else. Oh, now I remember." If this seems extreme, you may not have recently suffered yourself the normal disorganization that strikes most of us following a loss. We stand in the grocery store, mind blank, forgetting why we are there. And we use auditory recall, visual images, and lists to help us out.

Lists are another good concrete tool to help children with routine. Younger children can draw pictures to remind them of the tasks to be completed before bedtime or before the school bus arrives. These pictures or lists can then be posted in a logical spot, above the bed or alongside the front door, for quick review. They save the parent a good deal of nagging, and put responsibility back on the child in a way that recognizes his legitimate preoccupation with the loss.

Some children who are avid readers add a slightly different twist to this stage: they escape into books. The teacher complains that the child does not complete classroom assignments, preferring to read instead. At home, the child reads during the time needed to complete routines like getting ready for school or meals. Try making physical contact with such a youngster, touching a shoulder, then speaking the child's name: "Susan, it's time for school." And it may be necessary to remove the book. The adult who allows the child to "finish this page" is showing flexibility, but he may need to remind at the end of the page, before another seductively unread one beckons.

You may be recognizing parts of your own childhood as you read about this stage of disorganization. All of us have had trouble focusing on our daily tasks and responsibilities at times; and it can be illuminating to think about such a time in detail. When we do this we are often surprised to note that we too suffered a loss—not necessarily of a caretaker, but perhaps of a friendship, or some other childhood loss through a move or another event. In fact, throughout this book you will note that the grieving child does not become abnormal. She does the same things most children do; the difference lies in the frequency or intensity of the behavior. The grieving child may have some difficulty much more often or in a much more distressing manner than most children her age; or, conversely, she may never show the normal difficulties she should be having—a subject we will discuss in later chapters.

Despair

This may be the most difficult stage of grief to experience or to witness. The bereaved person sinks into a hopeless, bleak state of mind. The worst possible thing that could happen has happened, he thinks, and he is helpless in the face of it.

Like early grief, this stage often involves physical symptoms that indicate the level of stress and fatigue being experienced. In addition, the normal interests of living, eating, grooming, socializing are all diminished. It becomes difficult to rise in the morning and face another day. The child may be slower in speech and movement, pessimistic, and lacking in energy or motivation. He may think of suicide as a way of ending the pain and rejoining the lost person, or as a dramatic way of calling the separated loved one to return. Though rarely acted upon, these thoughts exist in many children.

Food becomes important to some children during this stage; they eat and eat as if to fill up the emptiness they feel inside themselves. Other children begin to hoard food, secreting it in their rooms or furniture. If you are dealing with a child who overeats, watch to see whether he keeps helping himself to food or whether he is taking it when it is offered. If it is the latter, you can help by serving food on individual plates rather than passing it at the table. If you give the child more than you think he really needs and he still asks for more, try helping him differentiate between the feeling of hunger and the feeling of emptiness. "I wonder if you're really hungry," you might say. "Let's try a snuggle [a hug, a backrub] instead." One caution: if you have not previously cared for a child of this age, particularly if he is an adolescent, you may not really know how much food he needs. If a child's weight does not concern his pediatrician it should not worry you. Many children, particularly teen-agers, can consume amounts of food that would make an adult ill.

Other children react differently to food, losing their interest in eating. In this case, offering foods they associate with nurturing, as we discussed earlier in this chapter, may be useful. Another technique for both heavy and light eaters is to teach the child to cook. This helps the heavy eater realize that he can begin to care for himself in a grown-up, nurturing way, which helps lift some of his feelings of helplessness and hopelessness. It also reinterests the light eater in food, and it allows any child to control what kind of food is offered at least some of the time.

Fortunately, for most children this difficult stage of grief is short-lived. Often it will last only about ten days to three weeks. If it persists much longer, it usually indicates that the child is having trouble getting the internal healing mechanisms going, and professional help may be needed. In adolescents as in adults, however, this stage may last for two or three months. Again, professional help is useful if it goes on longer.

The helping person should not be frightened of the child's

sudden helplessness and dependency. The adult's protective presence and willingness to share the child's feelings will sustain the child and keep him from feeling abandoned, isolated, or hopeless. But you should know that there are limits to what you will be able to do. You can validate the child's helpless feelings, but you cannot spare him his pain.

Reorganization

Jerome seems to be in a much better frame of mind than he was several months ago. He shows a marked decrease in his angry outbursts and irritability, and there has been no crying over his loss in a good while. It is not as if he has blocked out the loss, but rather that he has come to grips with it. His fifth-grade teachers report an outstanding change in his self-control, attentiveness, and performance. He seems both to understand himself again and to be more sensitive to others. After eighteen months, Jerome has reorganized himself to begin life without his missing parent.

In reorganization there are many steps, sometimes even leaps, in the ability to cope. You will see the child begin to think or act in ways that indicate that the loss has been surmounted. The child is able to invest in a new life, one that takes the loss into account but is not preoccupied with it. He is more autonomous, but also more able to become attached to others once again. He does not discount either his own ability or the helpfulness of others. Often the child seeks to find meaning in the loss, to fit it into his understanding of life, of God, or of what is good.

PHASE THREE: INTEGRATION OF LOSS AND GRIEF

For the fortunate child, the experience of separation or loss is mastered efficiently. The child reorganizes herself to get on with life. It is as if she says, "The worst possible thing that could happen did happen, and I survived it. Now I'm ready to get back to the business of living and growing." You will see such a child return to physical and psychological well-being; she will accept the reality of the loss, and her tears will be less frequent and less profuse. The child's self-esteem will be restored; and she will be able to enjoy life and other people, and to focus on the present and the future instead of the past. Often she will express a pleased awareness of having survived a challenge, having grown through the experience. Pain has been replaced with feelings of poignancy and caring.

For many children, though, additional help is needed before they show such positive integration of their loss. Such children may remain angry or depressed, or become inexpressive of their feelings. They may lack the ability to become involved with others, or stop developing as they should, or become preoccupied with physical aches and pains. They may become unusually vulnerable to new separations. You may find yourself having trouble controlling such a child, or see him become helpless and give up. Or the child's self-esteem may show marked impairment; he may discount himself and his feelings, underachieve, or behave destructively towards himself or others.

The remaining chapters in this book will discuss ways to help a child like this, who has finished the first round of grieving but who is still encumbered by what has happened. The helping adult can use many techniques to make it easier for the child to reorganize his life in a positive way.

3.
Sadness, Anger, and Aggression

ONE TASK IN RESOLVING loss and separation is working through strong feelings of sadness and anger. Many children, however, have difficulty doing this because they are afraid to vent these feelings or do not know what is allowed. This is partly because children often have little experience with mourning adults; they lack models to show them how to deal with grief. Or there may be no traditional mourning rituals for the loss they must undergo, as in divorce or a move from one family to another.

Some children have difficulty because of their past experiences with feelings of sadness and anger. Tears, for example, usually result from experiences in which the child was in some way vulnerable—injury and pain, fear, separation, rejection, being lost—so children frequently connect crying with feeling vulnerable. In addition, tears are often met with disapproval and censorship from adults and peers alike. "Don't cry, you're a big boy." "Crybaby, crybaby." The bereaved child's loss has already made him vulnerable, and he may avoid crying or other expressions of sadness as a way of protecting himself from internal feelings of weakness and external criticism and attack.

When grief causes anger, problems result because many children have found that angry outbursts may lead to additional trouble. Children learn early that anger is contagious. If you yell at your parent, he is likely to yell back louder and longer. He may even swat you or punish you. When a loss or separation removes a source of adult protection, children are often reluctant to risk bringing anger upon themselves by voicing their anger. Many children, too, are frightened by the potential destructiveness and power of their anger. Accustomed to magical thinking ("step on a crack, break your mother's back"), they fear that if they let out their rage after a loss some calamity may result. They imagine retribution, abandonment, desertion, injury, or even death to a loved caretaker, either absent or present, as the consequence of their fury. It is not uncommon for the sadness and anger following a loss or separation to be so strong that the child fears that if he gives in to these feelings he will lose control— destroy himself, damage someone, or go crazy.

Children also fear embarrassing, disgusting, or displeasing others. The child who is frightened by the loss of an important adult is particularly likely to try to please current caretakers at all costs. She swallows her sad or angry feelings out of fear that their expression will drive the caretaker away. The caretaker may contribute to the child's anxiety by sending subtle messages that sadness and anger are not permitted. Overburdened by his own feelings and new responsibilities, the caretaker may find the addition of the child's feelings overwhelming. He may feel somehow responsible for the loss and may need the child to validate his actions or decisions by acting untouched or even relieved. Or, having few remaining supportive resources, he may turn to the child for comfort and nurturing, thus denying the child's own needs.

Finally, many children who have been separated have a storehouse of anger resulting from their feelings of betrayal by those best loved and most trusted. They may show such obvious needs to retaliate, to strike out at those who have caused so much pain, that the adult is intimidated and anxious.

DECIDING WHEN CHILDREN NEED EXTRA HELP

Adults who work with grieving children sometimes need guidelines to tell them when the child may be in difficulty around sadness or anger issues. For the first six to eight months children are immersed in their own style of mourning. This may involve much denial and disbelief, much sadness and anger, or a combination of these. As the first anniversary approaches, the child who is resolving grief will have fewer episodes of anxiety, sobbing, and angry or destructive outbursts. After that time it is helpful to look at how the child behaves when distressing or frustrating things happen. Children who are in difficulty seem to respond primarily in two ways: they do not express feelings of sadness or anger in situations where most children their age would, or they express much more sadness or anger more frequently or in situations where other children are less upset.

Checking Out Problems with Sadness and Anger

Joann Burns left her husband some time ago. At first she and her two children lived with her parents; now they are sharing an apartment with her friend Don. Joann feels that she has finally found a relationship that is good for her and the children. But she is concerned with nine-year-old Jeff, who resists doing anything he is asked. He constantly stalls and complains. A conference with his teacher confirms that this is happening a lot at school, too. In fact, Jeff's teacher tells Joann that unless Jeff buckles down he will end up repeating third grade. Feeling frantic, Joann decides to get some outside help.

"Tell me a little about Jeff," the counselor Joann is referred to asks. "What kinds of things make him sad?" "It's funny," Joann answers slowly. "I don't really know. Oh, he gets mad, especially at his little sister, but sad . . . Even when I spank him he never cries." "Does he ever talk about feeling sad?" the counselor inquires. "No—even when you can tell his feelings should be hurt, or when he's probably really disappointed, he just sort of shrugs it off and says, "I don't care. Do you think that could be a problem?"

Both Jeff's mother and the counselor would be wise to check with Jeff to see if he can own and share a wide range of feelings, including sadness. Often this can be done by asking the child directly, "How did you feel when your mom decided not to live with your dad any more?" Or indirectly, "What would you tell someone about how kids might feel when they don't live with one of their parents any more?" Permission to express the feelings might need to be given. "Lots of kids have told me that they had some really strong feelings when they stopped living with their dads. Was it that way for you or was it different?" The discussion might be made easier through use of a book such as *Divorce Is a Grown-Up Problem*, by Janet Sinberg. As the pages are turned to show how a child feels about his parents' separation, Jeff could be asked if he felt like the child in the book or differently. A child who can talk about angry and sad feelings when such an approach is used is probably not burying his feelings inappropriately. Other children will refuse to discuss their feelings; one child drew a sign while her helper was trying to engage her in conversation. "No Talking in School. Priavisie," it read.

Five Feelings Technique

Many children are uncomfortable or unpracticed in talking about their feelings. When asked about them, they may respond, "I don't know." This may be a legitimate answer. It may also be an easy answer that means, "I don't want to talk about it," or "I don't know how to tell you." You can make talking about feelings easier by saying, "This doesn't have to be so hard. There are five most common feelings that grownups and children have: sad, mad, glad (or happy), scared, and lonely. Let's check it out. When you think about living with your dad any more do you have any sad feelings?'' ''What about scared feelings?'' And on through the list. This greatly helps a child to talk about feelings generally and also provides a way for the child to express mixed feelings, which many children find confusing and difficult to share.

If you use this technique, you should know that children can often show how they feel more clearly than they can talk about it. As you ask the child, ''Did you have any sad feelings?'' watch carefully for body signals such as nodding or shaking the head, or shrugging the shoulders (which often means ''I'm not sure'' but may also mean ''I don't want to tell''). You can then mirror back the physical signal and give words to what the child is communicating physically. ''Some sad. Okay.'' If the response was a shrug, you can say to the youngster: ''When I asked you if you felt any sad feelings your shoulders went like this. I'm wondering if that means that you don't know?'' A second shrug usually means ''I don't want to talk to you about this.''

Another useful technique helps you gauge the depth of the child's feeling by prompting her to show with her hands how much of the feeling she experienced. A lot would be hands spread wide apart; a little would be hands held close together. You can then put words to the child's physical communication. ''Did you have any sad feelings?'' You spread your hands and say, ''A lot?'' Bringing them together: ''A little?''—or something in between. ''How about lonely feelings, were there some of those? A lot, a little? I understand. You had or have a lot of sad feelings and a little bit of lonely feelings.'' And so on through the list. With adolescents it is useful to ask, ''How would you rate that on a scale of one to ten?''

Sometimes you may need to add other emotions to the basic list of five. Common ones are mixed-up feelings, silly or giddy feelings, embarrassed feelings, and helpless feelings. Many times these additions will be suggested by comments from the parents or teachers on how the child has reacted to the separation or loss. Other times they will arise in conversations you have with the child.

The Five Faces Technique

An excellent way to begin talking about feelings with a child is to use an activity that combines seeing, hearing, and doing, such as the "five faces" technique. In this way all avenues of communication are combined. An early conversation might sound like this:

HELPER: Hi, Jeff. We've got a lot of things we can do together. I thought I might teach you a game I know if you'll help me make the pieces we need. First we need to tear some pieces of this construction paper. What color should we use?

JEFF: I don't know. Blue, I guess.

HELPER: Sounds good. Okay, let's fold the paper in half and tear it along the line. Now in half again. [If helper and child each tear one sheet, you'll end up with eight pieces. If the child is reluctant to be involved, the helper can do the tearing for both.] Now we're going to make some different faces on these pieces of paper. You know, many times when people have something to say they show you with their faces instead of telling you in words. What about you, do you ever do that?

JEFF: I don't know.

HELPER: Well, think a minute. How would your face look if I told you that we were going to take the day off and just do something that was fun? I see. [Then you might want to copy the face with your face.] Your mouth would go up and your eyes would look like they were smiling. Let's try another one. What if I said that everybody but you got to take the day off and have fun, but you had to stay in and clean up your room? Oh. That would look a lot different. Well, in this game, first we have to make faces for different kinds of situations. Can you write the words for the different faces on these paper pieces if I tell you what they are? Good.

[JEFF, following directions, writes *sad, mad, glad* [or *happy*], *scared,* and *lonely*, one word across the top of each piece.]
HELPER: Good. Thank you. Now we need to make faces to go with the words. Which one shall we do first? [If the child selects the order, interesting information often becomes clear, such as which feelings are strong and which are avoided.] You picked *happy*. Will you draw it or shall I?
JEFF: I will. [He draws a face.]
HELPER: Great. Now which one?

Helper and child can proceed through the drawings, which will usually look something like this:

SAD   MAD   HAPPY   SCARED   LONELY

If you are stumped as to how to draw a face, or if the child is confused, try having the child show you with his face what he does with that feeling and then draw it. Or show the child how your face looks with that feeling, and have him draw it.

Children who have trouble sharing their sadness will give clues to the helper through their drawings in this game. "Your sad face is hard for me," Jeff's helper said. "It looks almost like your happy face [or angry face, the other common variation]. Is that how you look when you're feeling sad [an opener to good conversation]? I'll show you what a lot of people do when they have sad feelings." She added tears to Jeff's drawing. "Do you ever look like that?"

From these conversations clear diagnostic information often emerges. Children show which feelings they restrict and which act as a substitute for other feelings. Even if the child only watches and the helper does most of the talking and drawing, the child may progress: he learns that feelings and their expression can be safely discussed with this person in this place. At the end, the helper might ask, "Are there any other faces you think we need?"

Playing Games with the Feelings Faces

Several variations of games can be used with the faces to encourage further conversations about feelings:

1. *Pick a Card.* Hold the drawings with their backs to the child and ask him to pick one. Then the child can either talk about a time when he had that feeling or tell a story about what might make someone have that feeling.

2. *Fish.* For this game you need three or four sets of faces, usually including the set you have made together and others prepared earlier by the helper. Shuffle the cards and deal five to a person. Then play the game like "Go Fish," except that when a pair is laid on the table the player with the pair must tell about a time he had that feeling.

3. *Storytelling A.* Make up a story, tell part of it, and then have the child point to which feeling comes at that place. For example, "Once upon a time Gertrude the green giraffe woke up on a Saturday morning. She could see the sun shining brightly through her window. She jumped out of bed and said to herself, 'I feel so . . .' " After the child chooses the card, the storyteller continues, "because . . ." and goes on with the story. Or the child may draw a card and then be asked to continue with the story. What the story is about is not particularly important. It simply provides a nonthreatening way better to understand the child's experiences and feelings, to look for major themes (feeling left out, feeling anxious, and so forth), or to gauge which feelings the child avoids or returns to again and again.

Storytelling B. In this game you tell a short made-up story, stopping at episodes when a character might have strong feelings. Ask the child to point out the face that goes with events in the story. Then ask, "What do you think Gertrude [or the major character] could do to make things better?" This helps you understand better what the child knows about defending or helping himself, in what ways he feels helpless, and what fantasies he may use to handle the feelings brought about by loss and separation.

THE CHILD WHO BURIES SADNESS OR ANGER

Checking Out Family Rules about Feelings

One of the responsibilities of the helper working with a child who represses sadness and/or anger is to determine what part, if any, the child's caretakers play in such repression. If, as previously discussed, the caretaker sends direct or indirect messages to the child that particular feelings are unwelcome and may have damaging results, the helper must respect that the child is following a household rule. It is useful to know the caretakers well enough to have asked them, either privately or in the child's presence, what the rules are for expression of strong feeling in their family and what styles of expression are allowed. Holding a family meeting for this kind of discussion often makes clear to the helper who makes the rules about expression of feelings, who enforces them, what happens when rules are broken, how comfortable the parents are with their own feelings as well as the child's, and what the child is frightened may happen if he lets a particular feeling out.

Often it is extremely helpful to involve the parents in the work of assessing feelings that has been discussed in earlier sections of this chapter. The helper can watch for glances exchanged between child and parent as different feelings are discussed or faces drawn. "I noticed you looked at your mom just then. I'm wondering if you think it's okay with her for you to feel angry?" Or, "I noticed that David looked at you when we started talking about scared faces, Mr. Sadler. Maybe he's wondering how you feel about him sometimes having that feeling. Could you tell him whether that's okay with you or not?"

Another conversation that helps establish guidelines for discussion and display of strong feelings might go like this: "Mrs. Jensen, Peter and I have been talking about the kinds of things that might make him or a boy like him have different feelings. I'd like to ask you what people do when they have these feelings in your family. I know that everybody has some things that bother them or make them angry. Can you tell me what Peter is likely to do when he feels mad?" "You're saying that he most often cries and runs to his room. Thanks, it helps me to know that." "What about your mom, Peter? What does she do when she gets mad?" "Is he right, Mom?" "Okay, sounds like you've been watching each other and you know that both of you get mad sometimes, and that each of you has certain things you most often do when you're angry. Now let me ask you, Mr. Jensen, what about you? Do you sometimes get mad, too? Well, what do you do?"

This kind of dialogue not only gives the helper a sense of family patterns and rules about dealing with anger (or any other feeling that needs to be discussed) but also establishes that members in the family can watch each other, be aware of each other's feelings, talk about their actions openly. Even in families that usually avoid emotionally laden conversation, new permissions can be shared. If there appear to be strong rules against expressing, noticing, or remarking about feelings and reactions to feelings, the helper can encourage the family to experiment with doing so in this special time together or this special place.

If you are a parent trying to help your child through such conversations, it is extremely important—especially if no helping third person is involved—that the parents use none of the information shared by the child in one of these sessions to embarrass, control, or demean the child in any way at a later time. If the parents are also sharing their own feelings, whether a helper is involved or not, the likelihood of this happening is quite small.

If in the conversation one family member or another is unable to report on what she does when something engenders a particular feeling, it is useful to ask that person and the other family members to watch so that the information can be shared at a later date. This could eventually lead into a discussion of how one or another family member has a strong rule that denies that feeling and how their rule came into being. Was it learned from a parent or from something else in the person's life experience?

You may also find openings to point out that the child's troublesome behaviors are actually expressions of feeling, disguised either from the parent or from himself. Most parents can clearly recognize when a child is sad following a loss or separation. But if the child has a short attention span or is overactive, aggressive, or destructive, many parents will not connect this behavior with loss. Evidence shows that children who respond in these ways commonly have or have had parents with little understanding or sympathy for the desire for love and care, either their own or their children's. "After a loss, therefore, these parents are extremely likely to stifle their own grief and to be especially insensitive to how their children are feeling" (Bowlby III, p. 361).

Helpers, too, should guard against inhibiting the child's expression of feelings that the helper may have trouble experiencing personally or accepting in others. Bereaved children are particularly sensitive to verbal or nonverbal signs that the helper is uncomfortable with their expressions of feeling. A lapse of attention, hurried attempts to comfort, a flush, a shiver, or too quick a looking away can squelch such sharing immediately.

Connecting Actions with Feelings

One of the values of these family conversations is that they begin the process that connects feelings with their physical expression. For most people, just talking about feelings is not enough; they also need a physical component in the release of feelings. This varies from crying to door slamming, but it is an integral part of working through the strong feeling following a loss or separation, particularly in children. The inexperienced helping person must beware of assuming that because the child can talk about her feeling she has finished her grief work. Some children learn to parrot the appropriate words about feelings in order to satisfy the helper, but never allow for the real internal experience and its release. Especially when a child is being moved from one caretaker to another, this kind of parroting is frequently part of denial, a defense system. If the child is able to talk about the forthcoming move easily, particularly if she talks about it in a singsong manner as if reciting something memorized, determine whether this child has indeed shown anyone some angry or sad feelings connected with the change. Grief, in children as in adults, is painful to watch. Since everyone is likely to wish the child might escape the pain, denial is often reinforced even by the very person who is helping the child work out feelings of grief.

Bringing Out Sad Feelings

Because feelings are so closely followed by physical action or reaction, it is not difficult to work with a child on both at the same time. One method useful in starting the flow of feelings to action is to involve the child's body in ways similar to those already discussed. For example: "Serena, you've told me that when your mom left you felt pretty sad. I was thinking that anyone would feel sad. I bet you looked sad, too. Can you show me a really sad face?" Or the lead-in might be different: "Serena, we're just getting to know one another. One of the things I've been noticing about you is that lots of times your face tells me things. Like I can really tell if you like doing what we're doing because you give me a big smile. But I bet you're like most kids. I bet sometimes your face says other kinds of important things about how you're feeling. Can you show me how you look when you're really mad?"

Many children will be able to do this readily. Others need more permission and a model before they can try, particularly if they have rules or fears about that particular feeling. If the child has trouble, the helper may want to make this activity into a friendly contest: "That's as sad as you can look? I can look much sadder than that. [Helper makes a sad face.] See if you can beat me. Hey, that's better. Bet I can look sadder. Now you try."

This activity may begin to release the inhibition. But sometimes it needs to be repeated. "You're getting better but you still need some practice." Often the child will begin to find the contest fun, and adult and child may end up both practicing sad faces and laughing with each other, a sure way to reduce the child's anxiety about expression of the feeling. A mirror can be helpful here, unless it makes the helper or the child self-conscious.

Once the child is able to make a sad face, the helper should add sound effects. "You're getting pretty good at that sad face stuff. Now I bet I can sound sadder than you—Waaaaaah!" The interesting part of this addition is that many children who have hidden away their sadness will tear once they make a sad face and add a sad noise to it. Their eyes begin to water, providing the helper a chance to move from the game to real sharing of feeling: "Ohhh, that doesn't look like pretend sad. That looks like real sad. And you've had some things happening that would make anyone feel really sad."

If the helper reaches out to touch the child with an arm around the shoulders or the chair, a hand on the child's arm or knee, or a hug if their relationship is close, the child may begin to cry or even to sob. The plug has been pulled; the child is ready for comforting. If the parent is involved, either as participant or helper, it is appropriate for the parent to be the comforter. For some children this will be the first time they have let their parent share in this part of their loss experience. If the parent is not involved or is unable to respond to the child's distress even when encouraged, the helper should provide comfort as best he can.

One of the benefits of this activity is that the child shares the tears. It is hard, if not impossible, to overcome grief by crying alone. The helping person, then, must be prepared to stand by the grieving child in this stage—not only physically at the start but also through the next three or four weeks, or sometimes even longer. Because of this need to be available consistently, this method of bringing out sad feelings should probably not be used by the professional who is about to change jobs, take a vacation, or be promoted. In addition, the helper may need to see the child more frequently at the start of this intervention. Parents can be invaluable here, whether they are the helper or are involved in counseling sessions, because they can be available to comfort when the sadness wells up between scheduled appointments.

Some children are very reluctant to cry in front of others. If they are "primed" for sadness and their tears are noted, they may be frantic to change the activity or the subject in order to keep control of themselves. This anxiety or avoidance can be noted with a suggestion to keep the child's sadness in the open. "I think you don't want to talk about sadness anymore today. Let me tell you one thing that I've heard from lots of kids. Sometimes people want to do their crying by themselves. They're not as likely to get a hug when they do it that way, but they think it works better for them. Kids who feel like that often tell me they save their crying for after they go to bed. Some of them say the shower is a great place to let the crying out; no one hears you and no one can tell afterwards." (Adolescents particularly seem to respond to the shower suggestion, reporting later, "I tried that shower thing; it worked," which may be all they want to share.)

Another way to bring up sadness is through the child's identification with another person or animal who has suffered a loss or separation. There are many good programs on television and in the movies with these themes. As the child or adolescent is moved to tears, the helper can make a connection between the pain the fictional character feels and its similarity to how the child may be feeling.

The helping person does not have to see the tears to know that the child is letting sad feelings out. There is no right way for grief to happen, and helpers should not demand more expression than the child is ready to reveal, or demand that it take a particular form. For most children and adults, though, tears provide a healing release and signal a need for comfort, alleviating some of the sense of aloneness and vulnerability engendered by the loss or separation.

Bringing Out Angry Feelings

Similar techniques can be used with the child who represses or hides anger. First the child is encouraged to look angry; then the child is encouraged to act angry; finally the child puts words to the actions. Again, the helper must be comfortable with expressions of anger and understand that many children need to act it out.

To invite the child to look angry, the same methods as for sadness can be used. To encourage him to put actions and words to his feelings, you might try something like this:

> HELPER: Dean, you do that angry face really well. I'm wondering what kinds of things make you angry.
> DEAN: I don't know.
> HELPER: Lots of kids tell me they get angry when things are not fair. Does that ever happen to you?
> DEAN: I guess so.
> HELPER: I have a mad game I sometimes play with kids when they have those feelings. It goes like this. [Takes large reinforced cardboard blocks.] You stack one block for the first thing you can think of. Come on, give me one. It's not fair when . . .
> DEAN: I have to stay in at recess.
> HELPER: [Slams block down.] I have to stay in at recess. [Holds second block.] And it's not fair when . . .
> DEAN: I get blamed for something I didn't do.
> HELPER: [Stacks block loudly on first block.] And . . .
> DEAN: [Louder] It's not fair when my mom likes George better than me. [Helper adds, "And . . ."] It's not fair that I always have to do the dishes. It's not fair that I never get to pick the program on TV.

As Dean thinks about his grudges, he is likely to find it easier and easier to enumerate them. If not, the helper can make guesses from Dean's past complaints, or can make a hypothetical stack. ("Other kids have told me they hate eating broccoli. And they've said, 'It's not fair that I have to go to bed so early.' ")

Now the helper says, "I'll tell you something fun to do. You look at that big stack of blocks and you kick them down, hard, like this!" As the blocks tumble and fly, Dean cries in glee, "Let me do it!"

Together the helper and Dean rebuild the stack, or Dean builds it alone. Prompted by "It's not fair when," Dean verbalizes his stored-up resentments, building his stack again and again, and crowing with delight as he kicks it down. Dean is taking charge of his release of feelings.

Within a week or two of such activities, Dean's caretaker reports that he is sleeping better and that he appears less tense and has more positive energy available. Dean asks in his counseling sessions, "Can we do some more mad games today?" When the time seems right—whether it is the first time the game is played or a session or two later—the helper may add with the final block on the stack, "It's not fair when someone you love goes away," or whatever fits the child's situation.

Children who do this activity with parents present may need to glance at their parents to check if it is okay for them to be doing it, as we discussed earlier under family rules about the expression of feelings. If the parents are waiting in another room, afterwards the child may immediately report to them, "We were being angry today." If not, the helper should take responsibility for informing the parents of the session's activities, so that the child does not leave guiltily assuming that he has done something wrong.

Passive-Aggressive Children

Some children hide their anger; others push it down inside, only to express it indirectly in what is called passive-aggressive (or passive-resistant) behavior. Because it is not directly expressed, the anger builds up; and the magnitude of the rage makes the child feel guilty. Consciously or unconsciously, she may begin to frustrate the adults around her, both to vent her anger and to get the adults to punish her and thus relieve her feelings of being bad.

Children who have suffered the loss of a trusted adult may feel betrayed. They may see themselves as pushed around or controlled, and want to get even. Their anger shows up as dawdling, forgetting, daydreaming, bed-wetting, losing things, breaking things, or "accidentally" hurting themselves or others. Bettelheim points out:

> The first freedom to retaliate reveals itself in hostile procras-
> tination. They do not dare to be openly aggressive, but they
> hostilely inhibit the actions and movements of the adults
> around them by not getting dressed, by losing things for
> which the adult must then search for hours, by slowness of
> speech or movements, by endless and meaningless stories to
> which we must listen, by blocking exits, or by walking so
> slowly or so immediately ahead of us that they reduce us to
> standing still. (Bettelheim 1950, p. 210)

Parents are unwise to react to this indirect expression of anger with the threat of punishment. It is more helpful to assist the child in bringing out her resentment and anger directly. The methods discussed in the previous section for use with children who hide their anger are equally appropriate for helping passive-aggressive children own and express their anger.

Managing Physical Release of Anger

When children get angry they seem to feel a surge of energy in one of three zones of the body: the mouth (they bite, spit, scream, swear, or want to); the hands (they pinch, poke, yank, punch, break, or want to); or the legs and feet (they stomp, kick, trip, run, or want to). The best way to help them physically release their angry feelings is to respect their energy zone and to devise a permitted expression for such feelings. It is easy to determine which zone brings the most sense of release by asking the child a question like, "When Susie told on you what did you do [or wish you could do] to get even?" If you watch the child as anger-producing events are discussed, you will often see the angry energy travel to the preferred zone: the child will begin to grind his teeth, bite his tongue, or speak cuttingly; or his hands will pick at something, tear it, crumple it, or wring each other. Sometimes more than one zone may appear involved, as in nail or cuticle biting. Try asking the child, "Which feels better, the biting or your hands?'' With feet and legs, the foot will begin to swing or kick at the air or chair leg, or the child may get up and stomp around.

Interestingly enough, if you explain this theory to children they are fascinated, and they will tell you straight out to which zone they think their energy goes. This may be the first time that what they do with their anger makes any kind of sense to them.

It is useful to have certain materials on hand to use as props in the physical release of anger. You may want to experiment with some such as these:

Newsprint, to tear, crumple, wad and stuff into brown paper bags for bopping or kicking with.

Clay, the kind used by potters rather than plasticine, which has to be warmed up and leaves oil stains. Wrap potter's clay in a damp piece of terrycloth and store it in a plastic bag for use whenever you need it; as it dries out a few drops of water can be worked into the clay. The back of a newsprint pad can cover the surface to be worked on, and small crumbs that spill can be easily cleaned up. Along with the clay, you might provide a rubber mallet, a table knife, a putty knife, or a biscuit cutter. Many children find working the clay, cutting it, pounding it with the mallet, and just splatting it hard against the working surface to be very satisfying ways to release their anger.

Reinforced cardboard blocks can be ordered from nursery or kindergarten supply companies and used for kicking and hitting. Small cartons are also good for this; if the helper has limited space a reinforced carton like those used to carry bottled beer may be wedged in the corner of the room for kicking. The child gets to release feelings, but the carton does not fly around.

Foam bats such as the inexpensive and durable Nerf Bat® hold up to much abuse and can be used to hit people, chairs, or blocks without causing damage. You can also make rectangular bats from foam cuttings available at mattress suppliers; wrap the handles with adhesive tape. If these bats are to be used on another person, three rules must be agreed to: 1) You may not hit anyone unless you ask them first and they agree; 2) No hitting above the shoulders; and 3) If anyone says stop, the game must stop immediately. With these rules in place even very aggressive children seem to be able to use the bats without losing control. An additional bonus is that playing with another person with the bats often alleviates not only hostility but also apprehension in both participants. It is common for a game to end with spontaneous laughing and sometimes hugging, both of which lead to feelings of closeness.

Punching bags and inflated clowns are useful to some therapists. The good punching bags are very expensive, though, and the others are constantly leaking. You may want to experiment to see if they fit your needs.

Jointed play people and animals like those made by Fisher-Price are sturdy and inexpensive, and can be supplemented with similar figures by other manufacturers to provide for additional ages and races. You might want to include a plastic dinosaur large enough to be used as a monster (preferably with open mouth and teeth), a Hulk-like figure, and a police car. Such materials not only help younger children play out their angry impulses but also provide a chance to replay their loss or separation experience, a primary method by which they resolve their emotional conflicts.

Be sure that you have enough play family figures to accommodate children who may have more than one household in their lives, as with stepfamilies or adoptive families.

Hammer and nails, and a stump or block to pound them on, are good tools for releasing anger. There must be a clear rule that the hammer is to be used only for driving nails into the stump, and its use should be restricted from the child who has problems controlling his impulses.

All these materials are useful not only to the helper, but also to others when the anger of children breaks through, whether it is related to grief, frustration, or heightened irritability following a loss. Schools would be wise to provide access to such supplies for bereaved children; many of them could settle down and work more productively if there were an approved outlet for their anger. Release can also be found in games such as tag and dodgeball and in races, unless the child is subject to ridicule in such situations, in which case the benefits are offset by the loss of self-esteem.

When a child has been working on releasing her anger physically with a helper who is not her parent, the helper should have a conversation with both child and parent to establish clear guidelines as to where and how the child may continue such expression at home. "Kim and I have been practicing letting out some of her angry feelings so that she won't feel so worried," you might say. "It seems that she could best use something to hit, and I'm wondering if there might be something that she can hit [or kick, or bite] and some place to hit it if she feels angry at home next week." Most parents will try to think of something that fits in with their rules—a rubber dog bone for chewing (a child can bite right through teething rings), pillows, beds, cardboard boxes, door slamming, or some aggressive outdoor activity.

It is important that the parents feel comfortable with what is agreed upon, whether the helper does or not. They may allow things in their house that you do not allow in yours, or vice versa. Parents need clear permission to ask the child to confine such angry expressions to the child's bedroom, or to leave a room if the child's venting of anger makes them uncomfortable. If the parent is clearly upset by the idea of the child giving physical release to his anger, it is probably better for you to arrange with the child that the games in which anger is physically released be confined to your sessions together. Different grownups have different rules, you can explain, and you do not want the child to ask for trouble. Children can accept this; they learn from their earliest years that what is acceptable in one place is not in others. A common result of telling children to save their "It's not fairs" and "I'm mad abouts" for you is that they arrive at the session nearly bursting. They can take such a restriction in stride, though, especially if they have previously hidden or repressed their anger.

Aggressive Behavior

The earliest outbursts of anger usually occur relatively soon after the loss, when the child is still in the early phases of grief. These will often involve hostility towards adults and aggressive behavior towards other children. The child lashes out in anger against convenient people who have remained untouched by the upheaval and are going about their lives as usual. He snaps at those around him rather than manifesting sorrow or pain. He becomes furious with the caretaker who reawakens awareness with words of support, or who does not provide what is truly wanted—a return to things as they were. In the company of other children he hits, bites, pinches, trips, or makes cutting remarks.

Many times such behavior modifies itself without intervention, disappearing as the child progresses through the stages of grief. In some bereaved children, though, aggressive behavior continues and eventually seems to become a basic part of the child's behavior pattern, causing difficulty with peers and adults alike.

When you work with a child like this, you should know that this aggressive behavior probably serves a purpose, meeting some need originating either in the present or the past. To coax, embarrass, threaten, or punish a child to change her behavior discounts its function. A better approach is to talk with the child about the ultimate outcomes of the aggressive behavior, so that she can find other ways to take care of herself.

Help was sought for Kareen, for example, who had moved at thirteen into a foster family and was posing problems now that school had started. Both at home and at school, Kareen seemed to have a chip on her shoulder; she had been kicked off her school bus after several incidents where she stuck other students with pencils. The first interview sounded something like this:

> HELPER: I heard that things were not going so well on the school bus.
> KAREEN: Yeah! Those turkeys can take their bus and stuff it.

HELPER: How are you getting to school? [Kareen had previously seemed to enjoy school and was doing well academically, so the bus suspension did not appear to be a way to avoid it.]

KAREEN: They [the foster parents] are driving me, but now they say they're going to make me walk, and it's four miles!

HELPER: How come you stuck those kids with your pencil?

KAREEN: They're a bunch of stuck-up weirdos. They think they are so great. Well, they can't push me around. I showed them!

HELPER: You did? How?

KAREEN: They give me their funny looks like I don't belong on their dumb bus and I got 'em. I stuck 'em. That'll show 'em, the turkeys.

HELPER: Let me see if I've got this right, okay? You have to get on this bus every day with a bunch of turkeys who don't think you are as good as they are, hm? That must make you pretty mad, hm?

KAREEN: Yeah!

HELPER: So when you get that mad, pushed-around feeling you want to get even and show them not to mess with you?

KAREEN: Yeah.

HELPER: So you stick them with your pencil?

KAREEN: Un-hunh.

HELPER: Small problem occurs to me. Who's off the bus?

KAREEN: What?

HELPER: Looks like you got even and they got you off the bus.

KAREEN: Oh . . .

Another such conversation took place with eleven-year-old Robert, who was spending many of his recesses in the hall outside the principal's office where playground monitors sent him because he fought with other children. Robert's helper respected that perhaps his fighting was a way of meeting his needs. "So maybe you just really like spending all that time with your principal. Maybe you're thinking you want to be a principal yourself someday, so you like to stick around and watch what he does?" she says good-humoredly. "No? Well, if you'd rather be outside with the other kids, it looks to me as if we might want to figure out why you need to hit them. Maybe there's some other way you can take care of yourself that doesn't end up with you being sent in to the principal all the time. Are you interested in working on that?"

In working with aggressive children it is good to allow for freedom of choice, since much aggressive behavior, especially in bereaved children, grows out of their feelings of helplessness. You should establish that their behavior makes sense and involves a choice, that they can look at their choices and decide what is good or fruitless about them, and that they can figure out more rewarding ways to meet their needs. This avoids the impression often given to these children that they are somehow out of control and cannot change—an impression that makes them feel even more threatened and helpless.

Setting Limits. The helping adult, however, may also forbid dangerous or harmful behavior. "What you are doing is not safe [or not good for you and others]. I want you to take better care of yourself." "When you have that hitting feeling *you may not hit Tim.* You may hit your pillow or bang your fists on the table." Setting limits in this way recognizes the child's feeling or need; gives permission for a sanctioned expression of that feeling; and allows for more than just one outlet, avoiding the conflict that sometimes follows when the child is told, "Don't do that [your thing]; do this [my thing]." When you see the child about to lose control of his choices, you can lend adult support, relieving the child's distress. "It's getting hard for you to stop. I want you to sit down or go to your room until you cool off." You can try to defuse the situation and provide for face-saving. "You think it is your turn; Timmy thinks it is his turn. You boys have a difference of opinion. Both of you want the next turn. How can we solve it fairly?"

Bridging from One Behavior to Another. Often, in order to change behavior, several small steps toward the ultimate goal are necessary. Because the aggressive behavior meets some need, the child needs time to give up one behavior for another gradually. It may be useless just to tell the child to *stop*. As in kicking the smoking habit, it helps to decide when the urge is most likely to occur, and then to plan substitute behavior to deal with the urge when the time comes. The quitting smoker, for example, often puts carrot sticks, gum, or candy in her mouth instead of cigarettes.

In the same way, children may need to adopt some similar, but less harmful, activity as a bridge when they are asked to give up aggressive behavior. The helper working with Kareen, for example, suggested something else Kareen could do that might take care of her problem without getting her kicked off the bus. "When they look at you funny," she said, "I want you to take out your pencil [current behavior], open your notebook, and write TURKEY, TURKEY, TURKEY in big strong letters [new behavior]. Then close your notebook and look right at them. I think it will drive them crazy." Children who have been hitting other children can be taught to make a fist and slam it into the palm of their other hand, which often encourages the other child to back down; or they might hit their own hip or thigh with a closed fist. Children who kick others might instead kick at the air, stamp their feet, or shift from one foot to another.

These suggestions provide for alternative activities using the current behavior in a slightly different way. The ultimate goal, though, is to bridge the child into a verbal venting of his feelings. So in combination with the substitute behavior, or as a next step, words should be added to the activity. Robert might be asked, "Are you willing to try something and see if it works to keep you from ending up in the principal's office? Okay, here's what I want you to do. When you have that feeling, try making a fist and pounding your hip, and say, 'I'm angry, I'm angry, I'm angry!' I'd like you to practice it now with me." If the helper models the new behavior and takes the child through it several times, he feels less awkward and it will be easier for him to re-member to try. He could be asked to report on how his new response works out, either at the next session or daily at home if the helper is a parent.

A child who strikes out at adults needs to be stopped with a clear directive, a recognition of his need, and some alternative activity. This may also involve physically restraining the child who is not able to stop himself. "Can you stop or do you need help? You're showing me that you need me to help you stop." Eight-year-old Carla, for example, had begun to show displeasure by pummeling her mother, who seemed helpless to stop her. The helping person showed how to take Carla's striking fists in her hands, saying, "You may not hit me; tell me when you are angry." At the same time, she moved Carla's arms back and forth in a hitting pattern, first in short punches and then in longer movements back and forth, which dissipated some of the child's energy and allowed her to calm down. The mother practiced with Carla, helping her express her anger verbally, which was better for everyone.

When a substitute behavior has been planned, agreed to, and practiced, the child may bridge herself from the physical behavior to a verbal or even a mental one. Such was the case with Kareen. When asked to report how the pencil and notebook trick had worked, Kareen, who was back on the bus without incident, said she didn't know. Every time she got the feeling, she said, just thinking about the looks on the other kids' faces if she wrote TURKEY in her notebook made her feel like laughing and she relaxed.

Parents need to be assured that thinking about doing something wrong is not the same as doing it. Frequently they can help their children by sharing fantasies they do not act out because the outcome would be bad or because they think such action is wrong. Most of us have fleeting pictures of ourselves acting out these fantasies in frustrating situations: "What I would have liked to say," we think, or, "If he does that one more time I'd like to . . ." The problem is that we internalize these processes. Our children never learn that we, too, get aggressive impulses—and they don't see what we do with them instead of acting on them, whether it be a mental conversation or an action played out in our heads. If parents begin to share some of their own internal defenses, children have a good model on which to base their own actions.

CHRONIC SADNESS AND/OR ANGER

In direct contrast to the child who needs help bringing sad and angry feelings into the open is the child who is constantly sad or angry. Tara, who is six, changed families several months ago. Her new mother complains that nothing seems to please her; Tara cries and moans and groans about everything. She cries when she is frustrated by a stubborn button or loose shoelaces. She cries about imagined slights. She cries on and on about the tiniest bump or scratch. She cries because "he was looking at me," or because it isn't her turn to sit by the car window, or because it is her turn to set the table. "You'd think she would rust," says her mother in frustration.

There is a chance that Tara has an internal rule, "Don't be angry." When she feels angry she may convert that feeling into an allowed feeling of depression or sadness. Some of her tears, then, come from genuine sadness; others stem from anger. Other children, frightened by the vulnerability of sadness, may convert it into rage, releasing their sorrow as hostility, irritability, annoyance, or complaining. Children who convert their feelings this way will appear to be immersed in sadness or anger; one mode of expression is used for two feelings.

The main problem with these conversions is that releasing a converted feeling has no effect upon the original feeling. In order to be released, an emotion must be brought out unmasked. When a conversion of feelings is suspected, the techniques described in earlier sections on bringing out sadness and anger can be a good approach.

Other children linger in chronic sadness or anger for a different reason. As the stress of their separation or loss makes them long to return to an earlier, easier time, and as they go through the yearning and searching stage of grief, they seem to come to a piece of magical thinking that is based on fairy tales. A great many fairy tales do involve losses; what is unique about them, though, is that the central character eventually gets what is needed to fill the gap left by the loss. In the Cinderella story, for example, Cinderella loses her mother, gains a wicked step-mother and two selfish stepsisters who exploit her, finds her father unavailable to her, and is forced to do everyone's work. *Finally,* when she has been miserable *long enough,* her fairy god-mother appears and enables Cinderella to meet the prince, al-most lose him, but triumph to live happily ever after. Have you ever wondered where that fairy godmother was during all those years of deprivation? The formula clearly established, in this fairy tale and in many others, is that in order to get what you want you must have a loss and then have bad things happen to you *long enough* that you have earned a happy ending.

Some children who seem stuck in chronic anger or sadness, then, may be using their feelings as a way of searching. "If I cry loud enough and long enough," or "if I'm angry enough long enough," they think, then someone will take them seriously and their wrongs will be redressed. So long as this thinking continues the loss is unlikely to be seen as permanent and hope lingers on. The techniques used to diminish denial and disbelief, which we discussed in Chapter 2, can be a beginning in trying to ease a child through this stage. In addition, gentle confrontation is a help. "You've been being really sad for a long, long time. I'm wondering how that sadness can be good for you. You don't know? Well, let me tell you what other kids have said and see if any of their guesses fit you. Some kids have told me that they think it might make [the absent caretaker] mad if they stop being sad [or mad]. Is it like that for you? [If so, the child needs work around permission to move on, as discussed in Chapter 6.] Other kids have told me that it's like a deal they make, where if they just keep sad [or mad] enough long enough they can make things different. Do you ever feel that way?" If this last is the case, ask the child if he thinks the deal is working. How can he tell? Sometimes parents can be brought into such conversations, so that the child can discover whether things can be changed by his behavior. "What about it, do you think maybe somebody could make your mom change her mind about the divorce?" you might ask, and explore the possibilities if this is so. "Sounds to me as if you are going to have to be a fairy godmother to yourself and fix up the things you can fix, so you can have some happier times."

Another helpful tactic is to point out to the child that he is using an awful lot of his time in feeling bad. "That doesn't seem very fair to me. I don't think you are being a very good friend to yourself. Seems like it must be about time for you to get a turn with some better feelings, think so?" Sometimes these conversations will release a child's hold on sad or angry feelings. When they don't, you might ask, "How long do you think you are going to need to be this unhappy? For ten more years? Five?" and follow with your wish, "I'll sure be glad when you give yourself a turn to have some more comfortable feelings."

None of these techniques should be used with a child in the early months of grieving, however. They are designed for use with the child who is still chronically preoccupied with sadness or anger eighteen months to two or more years after a loss.

4.
Making Sense
of Separation and Loss

ONE RESPONSE TO BEREAVEMENT in both children and adults is a driving need to make sense of what has happened and to understand the hows and whys that led to the loss. This comes partially from a need to restore order and meaning to the chaotic feelings that follow loss, and partially from a need to understand events leading to the loss so that further losses might be prevented. Children in particular ask themselves, "What's wrong with me?" or "What did I do to be punished like this?"

Because a great many losses experienced by children occur during their years of magical thinking, and because school-age youngsters and adolescents are likely to revert to this earlier kind of reasoning, a vast majority of children assume that they were in some way responsible for their loss. Many children decide, "I was so bad [in some particular way] or I was so unlovable that *even my own parent* didn't want to be around me."

These self-imposed labels "bad" and "unlovable" deal the child's self-esteem a terrible blow, from which many children are slow to recover. In addition, these labels often begin a pattern: the child acts out her understanding of just how she was bad, caretakers respond negatively, and the child's feelings of self-worth are further eroded. Some children become unable to respond trustingly to caring or affection ("How could anyone possibly love or want me when my own father [or mother] . . ."). A child who guesses that the cause of the separation was her wrong behavior may become stuck in the developmental process, unable to move past a particular developmental stage. Or the child may become stuck in a particular behavioral pattern, repeating it over and over even though the behavior is inappropriate and brings only negative returns. Unconscious guilt also shows up in acts of self-hurt, such as physical aches and pains, neglect of one's health, the onset of real physical illness, accident proneness, and self-defeating life choices in work and personal relationships.

If the child attributes the loss to "wrong" feelings, he may decide no longer to allow himself those particular feelings, or maybe even to avoid all his feelings. These decisions make it difficult for the child to deal with people or problems effectively. Instead of using the energy our feelings give us to work things out and to know ourselves, the child uses his psychological energies to deny his real feelings and often begins to respond to life in an uncaring manner. The investment in this decision can be observed in the energy such a child puts into the statement, "I don't care and *you can't make me!*"

A child who attributes the loss to wrong thinking often becomes anxious about her ability to think correctly. These children may become so uncertain about the validity of their thoughts that they have difficulty learning in school, making decisions, setting goals, or trusting their experience. Many of them seem to decide to "not think," and reinforce their decision by relying heavily on "I can't," "I'm confused," "It's too hard," or "I don't know."

Other children assume responsibility, imagining that by behaving or feeling differently they could have prevented the loss.

If you are working with a child who has suffered a loss or separation, one important task is to provide him with enough accurate information, in an understandable manner, that he can answer "how" and "why" in a way that makes sense. Such information relieves the child of blame, reestablishes his accurate self-perception, leaves his cause-and-effect reasoning unimpaired, allows him to progress in developmental tasks, and lets him go on to have good relationships with others.

Where Helpers Have Difficulty

Sometimes the adult available to the child is so angry or distressed about a loss that she is unable to talk constructively to the child about it. Other helpers worry that the child is too fragile, too young, or too tense; or they feel that they will rock the boat by talking with the child about the hows and whys of his loss. Sometimes the cause of the loss or separation is adultery, abandonment, abuse, criminal behavior, suicide, or incest, and the helper not only is personally uncomfortable with the cause but can't imagine how to talk to a child about it. There may be fear that the child will be compelled to repeat the parent's behavior, or that the child will be damaged emotionally if the real reasons are known. Or the helper may lack accurate information about what led up to the separation, and be confused or reluctant to interpret or intrude. You may also be concerned, if you are not the child's parent, about how that parent will respond to what you tell the child.

Unfortunately, such fears and well-meaning avoidance in a helper leave the child alone with his own fantasies—and these are often much more frightening, self-blaming, and damaging than the actual facts would have been. Robert, released for adoption at four by a single mother with three other children, responded this way a few years later to a discussion about where babies come from:

> ROBERT: Not me. I didn't grow in a mom.
> HELPER: You didn't? That's fascinating. You're the first kid I ever met who didn't get born that way. How was it instead?
> ROBERT: You see, what happened was one day my social worker was feeling like having a snack. She opened a box of crackerjacks. She looked inside and pulled me out. She said, "You're no prize!" and put me in the trash.

Is it fair to leave children like Robert to say these kinds of things to themselves?

ASSESSING CHILDREN FOR SELF-BLAME

There are a number of ways to determine whether a child might be answering the "how" and "why" questions by blaming herself. A helper might try any of the methods we will describe in the sections that follow.

Ask Directly

"So your dad decided he was not going to live with you anymore. What would make a dad do that?" "There you were, a little kid only this tall, and your parents just disappeared. Why would a mom and dad do something like that?" "So you were taking your nap and your mom got into her car and had an accident and died. Do you think maybe the accident had something to do with you?" Some children will blurt out their guess about how they brought the calamity upon themselves, greatly relieved finally to have have someone with whom to share their burden.

It is also useful to determine whether the child believes there is something else he could do, or could have done, to prevent the loss or separation. Again, ask directly in similar ways. "Do you sometimes think maybe if you could do it over you could fix it?" "Is there anything that you think could have made it work out differently?"

Observe Developmental Clues

The child's behavior, as you observe it and as it is shown in difficulties he has with caretakers, can help you assess whether he is blaming himself. As with sadness and anger, watch for feelings and activities that are avoided, or that are much more in evidence than in other children around that age. It is as if the child who loses a family member looks around trying to decide what it was he did to anger or displease that family member. Often a child picks a behavior connected to his age at the time.

Sam is two-and-a-half. His single parent breaks her leg in a fall and is in traction in the hospital. Sam is temporarily placed in foster care. If he thinks about what made his mother mad at him, he is likely to think of times when she was irritated with his saying "no" or "me do it" or with his toileting mistakes. If Sam believes that the separation happened because of his too-independent actions, he may become stuck in negative, controlling, or overcompliant behavior. If he decides it was a toileting problem he may continue wetting and/or soiling long beyond the time that most children have mastered toileting, or he may show marked anxiety when he wets or soils.

If Sam were three instead of two he would be working on slightly different developmental tasks, so his guesses about his separation might involve different behaviors. This phenomenon is often so striking that a helper may be able to judge from the current behavior of a child who is ten or fifteen that the child suffered a major loss at age four.

A good book to consult in determining out what types of behavior are typical to various ages and stages in child development is *Child Behavior*, by Frances L. Ilg and Louise Bates Ames. It reminds you that children do not necessarily do their developmental tasks on a particular time schedule; the speed is determined somewhat by the individual child. Children do, however, master developmental tasks sequentially; by getting a feeling for where they are in relation to others, you can better understand their individual tempos. If you find that a given behavior is abnormally rare or frequent, you often learn something about the child's feelings of self-blame.

One caution: The behaviors that signal self-blame seem most often to be developmentally connected. Occasionally, however, a child will make a coincidental connection, putting together two unrelated happenings and developing a reason for blame from them. Tony, for instance, was a kind five-year-old who was very little trouble to his parents. He did sometimes become angry with his two-year-old sister Yolanda, though, because she was continually intruding in his play. One day as he was making roads in the dirt for his truck she insisted on sitting on his nearly completed project. After calling to his mother for help to no avail, Tony hit Yolanda on the head with the truck, making a small cut that bled profusely. Yolanda screamed frantically, and his mother came running in great alarm. When months later his father left to seek work in another state, Tony's conclusion was, "What I did was to be aggressive." Without help, he might have developed into a boy who hit other children much more than most boys do, or one who was unable to fight back but brought down abuse from other children on himself. Similarly, a child orphaned in a tragic accident was asked why she thought her parents didn't come home as they had promised. "It's because of my [table] manners," she whispered very softly. "I'm really messy."

This is not to imply that part of the child does not hear and understand the real cause of the separation or loss. But the part of the child that thinks magically blames himself.

Ask Indirectly

Often in finding answers to these problems you will need to ask the child indirectly why he thinks the loss occurred. One way of handling emotionally laden material is to use an embedded question. Here the helper begins with a personal statement ("I'm wondering" or some variation), followed by the question ("What do you think might make a mother do something like that?"). Other openings: "I was thinking about what we talked about, and I was guessing what you would say if I asked you why a mother would do something like that." Or, "I'd like to hear what you think about . . ."

Another good method is to ask symbolically. You might offer some art activities and then ask the child to tell stories about his drawings.

HELPER: Today for my turn I'd like to ask you to draw me a picture of a house.

MARCY (age six): [On bright orange paper in green crayon, draws a fairly typical house, peaked roof, chimney, two sashed windows, and a front door. Sneaking a glance at the helper she picks up an orange crayon and colors in a pane in one of the windows. The color shows, but only slightly.]

HELPER: Looks like part of your window is different. Can you tell me about it?

MARCY: Yeah, it's broken.

HELPER: How did it get broken?

MARCY: The mother threw the doll out the window.

HELPER: Why would a mother want to do something like that?

MARCY: Because the baby was yucky.

Marcy, by the way, was in her fourth foster home. She had "broken" down three previous placements by what could easily be described as "yucky" behavior. This conversation provided a good opening for talking about her separation from her birth mother and relieving stored-up guilt. A caution: The helper is wise to always remember that the symbolism in children's art merely provides some clues. Unless you check your guesses about what those clues mean to the child, you may misinterpret or guess wrong. Go ahead and act on your guesses, but until the child confirms them they are not indisputable information.

Another source of symbolic information can be the child's play with the figures and props we discussed in Chapter 3. To the play figures the helper may want to add a van with a sliding door that opens, which can be used for the play people and their possessions; a stove, sink, and refrigerator; table and chairs; beds; toilet; and whatever else seems helpful. It is important not to direct the play, but if the same pattern presents itself repeatedly and its meaning is not clear, you might say, "I see that the dad is leaving again. How do you think [some character in the drama] feels? How do you think Dad feels? [Some character] is watching the dad leave. What do you think she feels? Is there some way she could make things change?"

A final technique for helping children communicate their blame symbolically was first presented by Despart in 1946. This method, known as the Despart Fables and described in the American Journal of Orthopsychiatry, uses fables to explore the child's conceptions of the cause of the loss. For example:

The Funeral Fable (to investigate hostility, death wishes, guilt feelings, self-punishment): A funeral is going through a village street, and people ask, "Who is it that is dead?" Somebody answers, "It's somebody in the family that lives in this house." Who is it? For the child who has no conception of death, tell the fable in the following way: Somebody in the family took a train and went way, way far away and will never come back. Who is it? (Enumerate the members of a family.)

The Anxiety Fable (regarding anxiety and self-punishment): A child says softly to himself, "Oh, I am afraid!" What do you suppose he is afraid of?

The News Fable (To test the wishes and fears of a child): A child comes back from school (or a walk), and his mommy tells him, "Don't begin your homework right away, I have some news to tell you." What do you suppose the mommy is going to say?

Bad Dream Fable (for a check on the preceding fables): A child wakes up one morning all tired, and he says, "Oh, what a bad dream I had!" What do you suppose he has dreamed?

You can successfully use variations on the Despart Fables, such as, "The mom packs a suitcase. She is very angry. A child asks what is happening. The mom says that someone is going away and not coming back unless something changes. Who is going and what has to change?" Or, "A child hears her parents fighting. They are yelling loudly. What do you think the parents are fighting about?" Or, "Someone dies [or goes away]. Everybody thinks they know why it happened. But a child knows a secret reason. What do you think the secret is?

When you feel that the child is communicating confusion about events in her own life through symbolism, you can comment, "That's a little like what happened to you, isn't it?" or "I'm wondering if you sometimes feel like that is what happened to you?" Again, your guesses are just that, and should be checked with the child. If you are fairly confident of your interpretation, you might say, "It looked to me just then as if that were a little like what happened to you." If the child disagrees, you can either let the conversation drop or insert, "We have a difference of opinion about that, I guess."

MAKING SENSE OF PAST LOSSES

Sometimes you will have to help a child better understand a loss or separation that occurred some time ago, even years before. Perhaps the child was very young at the time of the loss, or the caretaker was so stunned that he had no energy to help the child understand what was happening. Perhaps the move was the result of a crisis, as often happens in foster care. Or perhaps the child has simply reached a developmental stage where questions about personal history are common—as often happens at around six or seven years, ten to twelve years, and in adolescence.

Sometimes the child's behavior or recurring concerns will signal the caretaker that the child needs help with old misunderstandings or confusions. In addition, grief is often cyclical; anniversaries, holidays, a return to old places or familiar situations, and the recombining of families may all nudge the child's memory and reawaken bereaved feelings. New losses, too, will not only add their own pain but bring up the pain of old bereavements, especially if they have not been resolved.

Telling Children about Difficult Information

You may feel awkward when you must talk to a child about the reason for a past loss or separation, because the cause is distasteful to you. Some of the common reasons that children lose caretakers, other than death or divorce, are abuse and aban-

donment; mental illness; imprisonment; incest; parental immaturity, rejection, or neglect; alcohol or drug abuse; and
suicide. "But how can you talk to a youngster about things like
that?" you may ask.

In such cases, an approach similar to the one discussed in
Chapter 1 seems to be both workable and helpful. Ask yourself:

1. Why would an adult do something like that?
2. What similar need or experience has this child had in her
own life?
3. How can this information be conveyed in a way that
places no blame?
4. Is there anything that the child might misunderstand or
feel responsible for, or any action by the parent that the
child might feel compelled to repeat?

With these questions in mind, let's take these difficult causes
of separation one by one, and go through the procedure that will
help you explain each to the child.

Abuse or Abandonment. The adult's reason might be
frustration; the parent finds that things seem too hard or not fair.
Relate this to the child's experience: "Does anyone ever ask you
to do something that is just too hard, or not fair? When that
happens, what do you want to do?" Most children will want to
get away from the situation (abandonment), or to strike out
(abuse).

The child might misunderstand or feel responsible in a number of ways. "It was my fault; I had too many needs," he might
think. Here you can talk with him about what children need,
making a list from things he knows about: bottles, dry diapers,
hugs, baths, and so on. Then ask, "Do you suppose that you
needed those things when you were little, too? Do you think it
was okay for you to be like all babies and need those things?"

Or the child might say, "I'm older now, so I can take care of
myself. If you just let me go back I'll be okay." Here you should
tell the child why it is not possible for him to go back, if this is so.

"When I feel that things are too hard I get away. Why did
they hit me?" the child might think. You might say, "Lots of kids

feel like escaping when things get like that. But other kids tell me they feel like doing something else, like hitting. Will you watch the kids you know and be ready to tell me which ones try to get away and which ones hit?"

Finally, some children say, "So my parents hit me. There's nothing wrong with that. Maybe I'll hit my kids too." Here you should say, "Kids are not for hurting. There's even a law that says that. When your father hit you because things were not going well, it was the part of him that had not finished growing up. Tell me, what are three things that he could have done instead? [Make list.] See, you are doing some work on the growing-up part of you, the part that knows what to do besides hurt kids." If the child cannot think of any alternatives, suggest some yourself to fit his particular situation; and review them with the child later to demonstrate that he is successfully learning alternatives to abuse.

Mental Illness. The adult's reason might be confusion about what was real and what was not. The parent may have had special trouble sorting out what was really dangerous, and might have felt scared most of the time. Ask the child, "Have you ever had a very scary dream, and when you woke up you weren't sure if part of it might be real?" Or, "Do you sometimes feel scared to go downstairs [or upstairs or outside] by yourself when it's dark? Do you think that maybe something will 'get' you? When those scary things happen, how do you take care of yourself?" Most children will report that they get a companion, check with an adult, turn on the light. Like the child, the mentally ill parent searches for protection from his fears; but the ways he does this make it necessary for him to be cared for by someone else, and also make it difficult for him to know how to take care of the child.

"Then I'll take care of them," the child might think or say. You can explain, "A parent needs a grownup to make him feel safe. You need to be working at learning the things someone your age is supposed to be learning, instead." "Well, I'll wait until they aren't doing that anymore," the child says. You can say, "All kids have things they need right now—like food, clothes, hugs, someone to have fun with. That can't wait. This is your only turn to be eight years old [or whatever age he is]."

Imprisonment. The reason here is that the parent broke an adult rule and is being punished in a way used for adults. "What are some of the rules at your house?" you might ask the child. "Do you ever break any of them? Then what happens?" You may find the child thinking, "My parent was a terrible person." Here you can say, "You know what lots of kids, especially little kids, tell me about breaking rules? They say that sometimes they just want something badly enough that they hope they won't get caught. I guess your mom was a little like a little kid in that way."

Incest. Here the adult's reason is often that he wanted to be close in a particular way. "Do you ever want someone to touch you in a certain place or in a certain way?" you might ask the child. "Like with a backrub, or a big hug, or a snuggle?" In the case of incest the child might conclude, "There is something wrong about sex." You can say, "Grownups do what your dad did because they want to be close in a special way that is fine for grownups but not good for children." Or, "Sex is okay when you are old enough. Like driving a car and staying up late, it is reserved for adults."

A child who has been involved in incest might also feel, "It was my fault because I did it [or I told]." Here you might say, "Your dad was the grownup, and he should have known better and stopped." Or, "Even if you liked what was going on, it was not good for you and the adult should have been more responsible. When you told, you helped him to do what he knew he should do, which was to stop."

Parental Immaturity. Here the parent was not old enough to have learned how to take care of herself yet, and found that taking care of anyone else was too hard. The parent may have looked grown up on the outside, you can explain, but might not have finished growing up on the inside. "Does anyone ever ask you to do something that is just too hard?'' you can ask the child. ''Do you think it will be easier for you when you are older?'' (If the answer is no, you can share experiences that other children have told you about.) Some children will misunderstand or take blame for their parents' immaturity; discussions like those described for abuse and abandonment will be helpful here.

Neglect. In this case, the parent may not have learned how to take care of children. Sometimes it will be obvious from the parent's history that this was because her own parents had not known how either, and hadn't been able to teach her.

''Do you think you will be a dad when you grow up?'' you can say. (If the child says no, you can say, ''Well, if you change your mind. . . '') ''When that happens, what kinds of things will you need to know how to do? What kinds of things do babies need from their moms and dads?'' (Make a list with the child.) ''Do you know how to fix a bottle, or change a diaper, or bathe a tiny baby?'' If the child says yes, ask, ''How did you learn that?'' Usually a child will have learned from watching someone else do it, or from reading books, or from seeing it on television. If the child says no, you can discuss how he might find out when he needs to know these things.

''My parent just didn't want to take care of me,'' such a child might think. ''One thing that is true about most grownups is that they really want to be good parents,'' you can say. ''Here are some of the ways I know that your parents tried to learn how to take care of you. [Name some: the parents consulted a social worker, hired a homemaker, took a parenting class, for example.] I guess it was a little like what you told me about learning to ice skate [or some other frustrating experience the child has shared]. Even though you really wanted to do it right and you tried as hard as you could, you just couldn't do it very well.''

Alcohol or Drug Abuse. The parent had upset feelings or worries, you can help the child understand, and used alcohol or drugs to forget them. This made it hard for the parent to remember to take care of the child. ''Do you ever wish you could just make your upset feelings or your problems go away?'' you can ask the child.

Some children will conclude, ''If you feel bad, take drugs; it makes your problems go away.'' You will have to explain, ''The trouble with taking drugs is that it makes new problems, it doesn't make your old ones go away. Have you ever done something bad and then lied about it? It's the same way: if you get caught you have two problems instead of only one.''

Check with this child, ''When you have problems or bad feelings, what do you know about making yourself feel better?'' You can point out, ''One of the things you are doing now is talking to someone to help things get better.''

Physical Illness. Here the parent is so sick that she needs to be in bed or needs to be taken care of. ''Have you ever been really sick?'' you might ask. ''Did it make you just want to rest? Sometimes when kids get very sick they find they don't even feel like reading or playing or even watching TV. They especially don't feel like picking up their rooms or doing chores. Your mom felt too sick to cook or clean or take care of things.''

In such cases the child may think, ''Maybe I'll catch what she had.'' Here you should explain if the problem is or is not contagious; and if it is, reassure the child that that is why he is not with the parent. If necessary, get the child a physical exam so that the doctor can reassure him that his health is absolutely fine.

Be careful also to make it clear that the child is not the cause of the parent's illness. (''I make people sick,'' he might be thinking.)

Parental Rejection. The helper will have to take special care when the circumstances of the separation involved parental rejection. This case, along with parental suicide, is often accompanied by self-blame that is stronger than usual in the bereaved child.

In the case of parental rejection, there may actually be something about the child that causes the parent to reject him. There may also be something in the parent's own life or background that contributes to the rejection, however. Your task will be to help the child understand which causes of the rejection are in the parent and which are in the child. Many children go through a stage of temper tantrums, for example, but most of their parents do not relinquish them for this reason.

The helper also must determine whether the rejection was precipitated by something about which the child had no choice. Perhaps the child was illegitimate, not of the desired sex, born at an inopportune time in the parent's life, of a different race, physically or mentally handicapped, or conceived as the result of rape. One approach that has been successful when talking about such cases is to ask the child, "There you were, a tiny baby growing inside your first mom. You must have known that she really wanted to have a little girl. Why did you decide to be born a boy?" The obvious unfairness of this line of thinking seems to help eradicate self-blame in the child.

Of course, the child should also be helped to understand that not everyone shares the first parent's feeling. "That mom knew that she found it very hard to feel comfortable with little boys. She did make a good plan for you. She knew that other moms and dads think that boys are special. Now you have this mom and dad. How do you think they feel about having you as a son?" It can be very useful to ask the caretaking parents in front of the child how they feel about him, to help the child validate his self-esteem in the particular situation.

Occasionally a helper will be talking to a child about a rejection that is, in part, an outgrowth of the child's behavior. An overburdened parent may have found the child's demands, outbursts of temper, defiance, or delinquency impossible to deal with, and made arrangements for the child to live with someone else. In this case, the helper should point out to the child that there are solutions to the problem. For example, together you can figure out why the child needs to behave this way and what else she might do to meet her need. Or you can offer assistance to the parent in understanding how to handle the difficult behavior, or perhaps look for a family that does not see the child's behavior as so serious a problem.

Finally, sometimes children have suffered a loss or separation in which little is known about the causes. This is frequently the case in families who have adopted a child from overseas, where the child may have been abandoned or separated from his parents in wartime or as a result of great poverty. In this situation it may be helpful to have a conversation like this: ''Most adopted kids sometimes think about their birth parents. You might wonder what they were like and why they didn't take care of you until you were grown up. No one really knows about your parents; none of us got to talk to them, so we can only guess. But I'll tell you why this happens to a lot of other kids in your birth country. It happens because there isn't enough money, or food. Or the family doesn't think they can give the child a good life. Or there is a war and people get killed. Or the child is of a different race and no one will help the mother. My best guess is that your parents' reason was one of these. What I'm sure about is that they didn't leave you because you did something bad or because you weren't lovable.''

Parental Suicide. The case where a parent has taken his own life presents another special situation in helping the child cope with a loss. First you need to explore the reasons behind the suicide: most commonly a feeling of desperation, the wish to seem important or to take revenge, or the wish to rejoin someone lost by death. Then it is crucial that you help the child to know what other things can be done when one has feelings like these. Many children who survive the suicide of a parent live for many years with the conviction that they too will kill themselves someday, according to Bowlby. The taboo has been broken; and in addition, the urge to rejoin the dead parent is strong. Discuss these feelings directly with the child, talking about the actions that can be taken instead of suicide to deal with them.

However, it is also very common for mourning children to think about dying as part of the searching and yearning stage of their grief. This is a normal reaction, usually evidenced in fantasies of dying by accident or illness; you need not interpret it as a suicidal tendency. If, on the other hand, you are working with a child who talks about suicide as a way of rejoining the dead parent, it is very important to refer him to a professional who has considerable experience with suicidal clients.

Studies show that there are several special difficulties in helping children whose parents have committed suicide. First, the parent may have threatened this action or attempted it before; and other adults or older children may have warned the child not to argue with or upset the distraught person. Such warnings and scoldings may encourage the belief that if the parent is pushed to take such final action it is because the child has somehow been the last straw. Bowlby points out that many such children hold themselves completely responsible, continuing to blame themselves regardless of what a helper might say. Such blame, he suggests, is an outgrowth of deep feelings of anger towards either the deceased or the surviving parent. The child cannot admit his anger toward the suicidal parent, because he is placed in a protective, consoling role towards her; and he cannot express anger towards the surviving parent because he is afraid of that parent's temper and possible suicide as well. As a result the child has no other choice but to turn this deep anger in upon himself.

Even more psychological problems are found, Bowlby continues, if the surviving caretaker bans any discussion of the suicide, or if he insists even in the face of clear evidence that the parent died because of accident or illness. Children in these situations tend to develop chronic distrust of other people, show an inhibition of curiosity, distrust their own senses, and find everything unreal.

The Death of a Sibling

In about half of families that suffer the loss of a child, one or more remaining siblings will develop symptoms such as depression, severe separation anxiety, and problems with going to school. This seems clearly to be the result of the changed behavior of the parents towards the remaining children rather than of the death itself. If the marriage founders due to stress, if the parents are depressed, or if the child's death is attributed to God's "taking" the child, there appears to be increased fear of being away from the parents. Something bad may happen to the parents during any separation, the child thinks, or they may decide to leave.

In many more cases than one would think, parents have blamed the surviving child for the death. This is most likely to happen in the event of a sudden death; and though parents often forget the accusation later, the child remembers and suffers a good deal of damage from it. It is good to check with the child, either directly or indirectly, to determine whether he believes his parents blame him, and to correct the impression if it exists by an absolving conversation between parent and child.

Making Sense Out of Multiple or Sequential Losses

It is not unusual for a child to have had several changes of caretakers. Such changes often occur following a divorce: children may be taken care of by grandparents or one parent until the second parent is able to make other living arrangements; or the custodial parent may have a series of live-in adult friends, as a result of changes in sexual mores. The child with overburdened or immature parents may spend some time moving from one relative to another. Or a child may enter the public welfare system and experience a number of moves from one family to another before a permanent arrangement is made.

Children may also re-experience a sense of loss when the finalization of an adoption cuts off wishes they have harbored to be reunited with their birth parents; when divorced parents remarry, thereby making the divorce seem irreversible; or when a child is born of the new union. If there are stepbrothers or stepsisters involved in a remarriage, and if the child's parent has custody of them while the child is only allowed to visit, the sense of loss is also deepened. Stepbrothers and stepsisters may precipitate yet another experience of loss by changing the child's position in the family, making him no longer the oldest, the youngest, or the only boy, for example.

Each of these losses creates another chance for misunderstanding, self-blame, and feelings of not measuring up in some way. It is wise, therefore, for the caretaker or some other helper to assist the child in understanding who these additional people are, why they came into the child's life, and why they departed if they are no longer available. Because this information is complex, helpers are often at a loss as to how to impart it effectively. How to bring up the subject and how to engage children who seem reluctant to talk about their past losses are usually the first two obstacles they face.

As is usual with children, a good place to begin is wherever the child seems to have the most energy invested. You can determine this by noticing what questions may have emerged from previous conversations, or by asking the child about changes in the past that may be confusing or only half-remembered. If the child has not broached the subject of past losses, or wants to talk only about the present, you may want to spend some time talking with her about who she is now—things she likes to do or hates to do, best friend, favorite color, how big she is, three wishes—before talking aboutpast losses.

Some children who have had outside helpers when they changed caretakers in the past may be apprehensive that you intend to make them move again. If this is not the case, you need to make that very clear: "I guess you know what happens after you come to see me. We have our turn, then we finish, then you go home. That is what will happen every time I see you. You will always be going home." If you will be involved in helping the child make another change of caretaker, though, it will be important that the child understand this role and that past changes be explored before making the new one.

Because children are so often fully convinced that they have caused their own losses, they are understandably reluctant to discuss their failures with a helper. If they have skipped over parts of their grief process, the discussion may reawaken old pain and confusion as well. So although many children are eager to find out "the truth" about what has happened in their past, even more want to avoid it at all cost. As you bring up the subject the child may feign indifference ("Who cares? I know all that stuff"), or divert you to another subject ("Do you know what my teacher did? It was really unfair. . ."). He may try to distract you by getting silly, falling out of his chair, inappropriately coloring on you or himself, or becoming very active either phsyically or verbally. Even if you are comfortable with such children and committed to helping them towards resolution, this resistance will be a challenge. They will take any tack to avoid dealing with the frightening and painful feelings connected with these past events.

The helper should adopt a compassionate but firm attitude in response to the child's need to push this information away. He might confront the child's reaction directly: "This is hard for you to hear. It makes you want to change the subject." Or he may want to cover information in small bits, leaving some time in between to share less demanding activities with the child. ("Today we're going to take turns. You get ten minutes to do whatever you want to do, and I get ten minutes to do whatever I want to do. Fair?") This technique is extremely successful, especially when used with a kitchen timer so the child knows how much longer the difficult activity will last. As anxiety-producing information is shared, some children will pick up the timer and begin to click it on and off; you should express your understanding of their desire to do something else, but insist that the turn be carried through to its end. Other children may become so interested in the information you are sharing that they will beg you to take a longer turn and finish.

The child may insist that he doesn't want to talk about what has happened in previous separations. "I know, I know," he may say, or "Why do we always have to do this stuff?" A good response to this child is, "That's terrific. I'm really glad someone helped you get all this straight. It makes what I need to do much easier. Can you tell me what happened so I can understand it? Then we won't have to talk about it anymore." Often such a child has a good deal of the information stored away. But usually there are pieces missing, particularly regarding the "hows" and "whys" of the separation, which have not been explained in a manner understandable to the child. Watch for the telltale singsong: "Well, you see, what happened was my father didn't love my mother anymore and they fought a lot. He left. Now he lives with Sue and Timmy and Beth and they are his family." By following up with the kinds of questions about feelings and magical thinking that we have discussed in the last chapters, you can uncover if and where the child needs help.

Adolescents who have been in constantly reorganizing family settings or in foster care are often very hostile when you bring up the subject of their past. You can arouse their interest in a similar way, by asking them to tell you their own histories. Usually they will relate in a bored fashion things like, "When I left my first family I went to live with the Thompsons. Then I left there and I lived with some lady and her son. Then . . ." "Wait a minute," you can interrupt. "Let's go back to the very beginning. You were born. When was that? [Birth date] Where? What time of day? How big were you?" For children with a somewhat chaotic background there is almost always some part of their history they are missing. If not, other questions can be asked in a matter-of-fact way. You will want to establish that you feel the adolescent is entitled to this information that other people know, and that you will help him get it if he wants it. "You know, John, most of this stuff is written down. I think it is your history and you have every right to know it. What do you think?" Adolescents are particularly interested in hearing what others have said (or written down) about them, and in having a chance to agree or set the record straight. Often their reluctance becomes real eagerness as they begin to understand background information better.

Helping Understand Personal History

Because the information being shared is often emotionally laden and quite complicated, the child needs additional help in taking it in and keeping it straight. There are a number of ways you can help the child to do this.

Respect the Child's Preferred Modality. There are three ways that people take in information, store it, and retrieve it: through what they see (visual), through what they hear (auditory), and through their bodily sensations (kinesthetic). As we mature and gain experience we become able to use all three of these; but in times of great internal or external stimulation we are apt to revert to our preferred modality, and to be most easily reached by visual, auditory, or kinesthetic stimuli.

It is easy to determine which modality a child prefers, and to use it when you communicate important information. Children, like adults, give cues as to which modality they prefer by the language they use when they are eager to make a point clear. By listening carefully to the predicates and idioms they use, you can understand and respond in the way that will reach them best. For example, in the visual modality: I *see* where you're coming from; *looks like* you're telling me; I *get the picture; plain as the nose on your face.* In the auditory: I *hear* what you're *saying; listen here; buzz words; music to my ears.* In the kinesthetic: *hang on* a minute; let me *juggle this around* a little; *get a handle* on it; *butterflies in my stomach; out in left field.*

This is easier to understand if you make a list for yourself of verbs, verb phrases, and figures of speech that fall into each of the categories. You will probably discover that it is easier for you to think of words in one of the modalities. This may tell you how you organize information yourself, which is helpful to know when you talk to a child about important background events. Like the child, you may tell stories in your preferred modality. If your style does not match the child's, she will have a much harder time making sense of what you are talking about. The best helpers become proficient in putting the same information into each of the three modalities.

If you are working with a visually organized child it can be helpful to draw pictures as you talk, in order to focus the child's attention on what you are saying. If you are working with a child who prefers the auditory mode you may want to use storytelling ("Once upon a time there was a tiny baby named Julie who lived in a house on a loud and busy street"), or pretend to be a television interviewer who talks to important people in the child's life with a microphone made out of a paper towel tube. Auditory children especially love to have sessions taped and important sections played back again and again. With kinesthetic children the whole body should be involved, in role playing, acting out parts of the story, and using play materials such as puppets or dollhouse figures.

Use Multiple Modalities. To have the most direct and efficient impact, it helps whenever possible to communicate important information with more than one system at a time. Some of the previously described techniques can be used to show the child what the event would look like, sound like, and feel like all at once. For example, you can draw pictures to illustrate happenings in the child's life, and have her tell stories about the pictures. Or you could stage a play with puppets or dolls, including lines like, "When Mary got up she looked around. Her daddy really wasn't there. She felt shivery and scared. She wanted to say . . ." The next few pages will describe a few techniques that can be used to combine all three modalities in helping children sort out confusing personal histories.

Time Line (for Younger Children). Tie a piece of yarn or sturdy string between two fixed objects such as chairs, furniture hardware, or thumbtacks on the wall. Using paper clips or clothespins, hang on the line small drawings or photographs of important people and sequential families in the child's life. The story might go like this: "First there were Pat and Allen. They met each other in high school and decided to get married. Can you draw me a picture of what you think Pat looked like? Okay, let's hang it here. Now one for Allen. Okay, he goes here. [Or you can draw the pictures, getting the child to tell you the colors of eyes and hair.] Then you came along, on May 16, 1978. [Hang picture of child next to those of birth parents.] When you were just big enough to be walking and getting into things the way all kids do, Sally was born. [Picture of Sally joins family.] But things were not going too well for Pat and Allen. Allen wanted to be out with friends much of the time, and Pat thought he should come home and help with the house and the children. They fought a lot. One day Allen just didn't come home at all. Pat was very angry. She was probably sad and scared, too. She waited for several days wondering if something terrible had happened. Then Allen called and said that he had decided to live with his parents and that he was not going to come home ever again to Pat and you and Sally. [Remove Allen's picture from the line and tape it somewhere else in the room, near of the child.] Pat decided that she would get a job to help with the money, and you and Sally and your mom went to live with Auntie Vi and Uncle Bill and their twins Allie and Angie. Let's make some pictures of them, too. [Hang these pictures farther down the line and move the cards for Pat, the child, and his sister, clipping them near the pictures of the new family.]"

Using this technique you can make successive moves quite concrete, talking about the reasons for them as we have discussed and incorporating a good deal of information in a way that the child can get straight. You can use different colors of construction paper for different birth families, to keep straight which children are biological children of which parents, something that can become confusing in remarriage and foster or adoptive families. You may also want to include the child's schools and best friends as they have changed along with the moves.

Try to gauge how much of the story to tell at a time by watching the child's ability to pay attention. When he begins to look spacey or to yawn, enough has been said. Better to change activities and do something fun, leaving the remainder of the information to be covered at another time.

This technique can be taken a step further by using the cards showing facial expression along with the others. After going through the history, you might go back to the beginning and do the story again, this time asking the child, "How do you think they [or you] felt?" For example: "In the beginning there were Pat and Allen. They met in high school and fell in love and decided to get married. How do you think they felt? [Happy.] Probably. They may also have felt a little scared, because they had never been married or had their own apartment before and so that was new to them. Then you came along, a handsome, healthy, intelligent baby. Now how do you think they felt? [Happy.] Yes, I'm sure they did. I bet they thought you were really special with your little fingers and toes. They may also have been a little scared because they were not used to being parents, and they wanted to do a good job. Allen wanted to work extra hard to make enough money to take care of you and your mom. When he finished a day at work sometimes he felt like going out and having fun with his friends." Proceed through the child's history, attaching face cards to the line in the appropriate places.

Time Line (for Older Children). With older children you might use a similar technique, but make it more like the time lines and graphs they may have used in school. On a large sheet of newsprint, draw out a time line and fill in the years from the child's birth to the present. You can use dates (1968, 1969, and so on) oryou can use ages (infant, one, two, and so on). Then go through the child's history, using a contrasting color to mark changes in caretaker or moves. A section of the finished time line might look something like this:

Tim born	Infant	1	Sally born	2	Dad left

Moved to Vi and Bill's	3	Moved to apartment	4

Ted moved in	5	Ted left	6

You might finish by talking about the feelings that accompanied the various changes in the family situation.

Storytelling with Houses and Figures. Pictures of houses can be cut out to hang on the time line, and faces drawn on them to represent who lived there. Or you may want to cut out pictures of people while you talk to the child, as a way of keeping him involved and interested. Taking your scissors, you could begin to cut the outline of a person or a house. "Today I'm going to tell you a story. I may need you to help me out. This is a story about a woman named Pat [cut her picture out] and a man named Allen [cut his picture out], who lived in a tall apartment house [cut it out and put Pat's and Allen's pictures on it]. After a while they had a tiny baby named Tim [cut out baby's picture], and about the time he was learning to walk they had another baby [cut out her picture and place it with the family] whom they named Sally." This can be done on a table rather than on a line, which allows for one individual to leave the family but still be in the story. Again, important friends and neighbors, schools attended, and remarriages can be included; and the exercise can be completed by discussing the feelings associated with the story.

After you have introduced these techniques of recording history, let a week or so pass and then ask the child to tell you the story. This allows you to find out what has been understood and retained and what is still confusing or misunderstood.

Making a Record for the Child

These methods of sorting out who was who, what happened when, and how and why are an excellent means of putting together a child's past and removing self-blame. If the helper is the child's parent and will continue to be available for questions, this is often enough for the present. As the child matures and gains more historical perspective, the parent can expect additional questions and a need to go back over and clarify the information. If a death has taken place, the child may take great interest in reading newspaper accounts or the funeral register again and again, to make more real what happened and the other people who were affected by it.

But if the helper is not the child's usual caretaker, some permanent record should be made of the child's history, so that he can review it whenever he wants to either as a reminder or as a means of understanding new information. Such a record also can provide a model for the caretaker, establishing some continuity in descriptions of past history as additional questions or comments come up in their life together.

The two most common ways to make these records are the *life story* and the *life book*, which can be given to the child or his current parents. In the life story, the helper writes out what she and the child have discussed together, including the reasons for various changes and the feelings that have accompanied these changes. In the life book, the helper brings together in a scrapbook or notebook pictures of the child at a young age, pictures of important people such as birth parents and other caretakers, and memorabilia such as might be found in a baby book. Again, a written description of who, how, and why goes along with the pictures. If no photographs are available, the child can draw pictures of important people, using whatever information is known or can be deduced. (Caution: Do not have the child cut out pictures from a magazine as a substitute for photographs. Magical thinking tends to turn those people into "my real parents," which only confuses the issue.) A good discussion of how to prepare a life book can be found in Claudia Jewett's book *Adopting the Older Child*.

If you are working with a child in foster care, a good way of keeping records is to supply each foster parent with a large manila envelope on an annual visit that might coincide with the child's birthday or the beginning of the school year. The child's name is printed on the envelope, and the foster parent is asked to save in it schoolwork, snapshots, awards, or anything else that keeps a record of the child's growth. In part because they wish to remain part of the child's memories themselves, most foster parents are very cooperative about this, and it makes your task of record-keeping much easier.

Bonuses for Making Sense of Personal History

It takes time to gather the information necessary to help a child piece together her past life experiences and make sense of the reasons behind them. But there are measurable rewards for doing so. Often a child who has been labeled hyperactive will reduce or stop her hyperactive behavior as the need disappears to run away from bad feelings or self-blame disappears. There is a significant decrease in separation anxiety, and it is not unusual for bedwetting to diminish or cease. Because of their increased ability to concentrate, children often demonstrate significant gains in their academic ability and performance. They grow in understanding of themselves; and relationships with others improve markedly as they stop discounting their own abilities. They are no longer afraid that their behavior or personalities will cause others to abandon them, and so they are more able to make emotional commitments to others. Such improvements obviously can change a child's life. Whatever energy you expend to complete this work will be well worth your time and trouble.

5.
Impaired Self-Esteem and Self-Control

THE LOSS OF A PARENT to death or separation strikes a blow to a child's developing sense of trust and self-esteem, causing feelings of powerlessness and shame.

If a child has had the good fortune to experience ongoing nurturing and responsiveness, she is likely to be trusting, confident, and competent. The longer she has had this base, the more likely she is to expect herself to meet life's challenges, and the more she trusts others to help her. She counts on the predictability of people, things, and events; her life has continuity and meaning.

When she is suddenly confronted by the loss of a caretaker, this foundation is greatly challenged. Her trust in the constancy of her caretaker's availability for support, comfort, and protection is shaken. She may become afraid to misplace her confidence by depending on others, particularly if the remaining caretaker, distraught and vulnerable, is experiencing insecurity, anxiety, and irritability—feelings that interfere with his interactions with the child just when she needs most to count on him.

If the child is under three or four, she will have had less experience with life's dependability, and she will be more likely to have difficulties following the loss. Periods of unstable substitute care, more probable at this age, often compound the problem.

The child may begin to fear that all her relationships will end in failure, and to view life as full of threatening surprises with painful consequences that she is powerless to remedy. She suddenly questions her outlook and mistrusts her perceptions. Her sense of life's benevolence, predictability, and meaning is lost.

A child who has never experienced a stable and secure relationship with a caretaker, or has somehow not learned to trust adults, is even more at risk. Perhaps the child has been repeatedly told that he doesn't measure up. He is likely to develop an image of himself as unlovable and unwanted. When he suffers adversity, he expects others to be hostile and rejecting rather than helpful. He stops believing that he can make and hold on to relationships, and this becomes a self-fulfilling prophecy. Behavioral problems that develop as he gets older may indeed put stress on his family and friends; and increased incidents of breakups, separations, and losses reinforce his belief that he will fail in making stable relationships. Children with such histories of hardship see life as comfortless and unpredictable, and tend to respond by shrinking from it or by doing battle with it.

Additionally, a strong sense of shame following a loss often makes the child feel unworthy and unlovable. Some of this is a result of the self-blame discussed in Chapter 4; feeling abandoned or deeply hurt, the child decides that "I was so bad" or "I was so unlovable that even my own . . . ." Instead of approaching life with high self-esteem and confidence, the child feels publicly exposed and censured. Mortified and humiliated, he thinks that everyone knows he has somehow disgraced himself. Some children exaggerate their inadequacies, confessing to one and all how bad and unlovable they are; others go to extremes to hide either themselves or the information about their loss. Some throw the responsibility for their shameful feelings onto others, becoming belligerent and aggressive.

These reactions are even more prevalent if the child is shunned, as many are, by other children who fear the reminder that caretakers are not always available. Much can be done to alleviate the school-age child's sense of separateness and shame. Often he will not be aware, for example, that other children in his classroom or school have also experienced loss and separation. It is helpful to pair the child whose parents are newly divorced with another such child for schoolwork; spontaneous conversations regarding the similarities and differences in their situations often occur. Schools would be wise to provide conversational groups, too, for children who have experienced loss. Teachers can initiate class discussions or study units about a variety of family lifestyles; include books for children about divorce and step-parenting among the classroom reading matter; and make periodic and casual mention of separated parents, single parents, and foster and adoptive parents. They should also be sensitive to holidays that some children may find difficult, particularly Mother's Day and Father's Day. And Stuart and Abt suggest:

> If a child with recently separated parents newly enters the school district, teachers need to be sensitive to the child's loss of peer support in addition to the parental loss. The child needs to feel a sense of belonging to the class and to acquire a new support system as quickly as possible. To foster this, the teacher could assign the child a valued responsibility, include the child on committees, have the class members plan a welcoming party or form a "Newcomer's Club," and a unit on the child's previous hometown could be done (p. 162).

Assessing Children's Feelings and Self-Blame

There are a number of ways to check for diminished self-esteem, shameful feelings, and powerlessness. Here are some techniques that work well:

Ask Directly. "I'm wondering how you have been feeling about yourself lately. If you were giving yourself a grade for how likable and good you were, what grade would you get?" "If you were giving yourself a number, with 10 being the best kind of boy and 1 being the worst, where would you put yourself?" Or, "Other kids have told me that after their parents separated they felt embarrassed and didn't want anyone to know. Was it like that for you, or was it different?" You may not even need to ask; the child may allude to, or claim directly, feelings of inferiority, separateness, and embarrassment about the loss.

Ask Indirectly. Observe how the child responds to praise and criticism. If you are not the parent, ask caretakers how well they think the child takes positive and negative comments. Find out if he has trouble making or keeping friends. Watch for the child's continual misinterpretation; does he assume that others don't like or approve of him, and act on those guesses a good deal of the time? One clue to what the bereaved child feels towards others can be found in the names he calls himself: "I'm no good. I'm dumb!" And conversely, names he calls others are often names he calls himself.

In *Getting to Know the Troubled Child,* Looff describes an exercise for exploring how the child sees himself. He asks the youngster to draw a person. Then he leads the child into conversation by saying that behind the good drawing there must be a good story. "Would you say that this person is a boy or a girl? A man or a woman?" "How old would you say he is?" "I guess he should have some kind of name; what shall we call him?" "He's probably like all boys. I wonder what he likes to do especially?" "Is there anything in particular he's proud about?" "Like all boys, he probably has some tough times. What might worry this Jimmy?"

Another useful way to get to know how a child sees herself and others is through playing "The Ungame" (manufactured by the Ungame Company, P.O. Box 6382, Anaheim, California 92806; available in toy and game stores). The game includes a variety of questions that establish common themes and perceptions in the child's life: "Describe a perfect mother; say something about a friend; share something that you fear; what do you like most about yourself, least?'' Much information can be shared in a non-threatening way.

Ask Symbolically. Watch the themes that recur in the child's play. Find out if she has a favorite story or TV character; see if there are any similarities to the child that might suggest attributes she wishes to own or outcomes she would like.

If you are a trained helper, try the House-Tree-Person series, the C.A.T. tests, or a kinetic family drawing.

The Bucket Theory. I often use the following analogy as a way of explaining what happens to a child's sense of self following a loss:

Imagine that everyone is born with an invisible bucket hung over his arm. Each interaction can be positive, leaving the person feeling good, alive, significant; or it can be negative, leaving the person feeling bad, numb, worthless. A hug is a positive physical exchange; a spanking is a negative physical exchange. Verbal exchanges include a supportive compliment or angry criticism. Internal comments would include the positive sense that "I can do most things well" or the negative "I'm no good." As a child receives good nurturing and approval, positive interactions stimulate positive feelings—self-esteem, confidence, trust—and positive energy flows into the child's "bucket."

When a child loses or changes caretakers, the bucket is "sloshed" and some of these good feelings about self and others are spilled. If the child has strong feelings of guilt and shame, he develops "leaks" in his bucket. Even if positive energy is available, the child's good feelings about himself and others are slowly drained out. Or the child may discount his need for positive energy or his ability to get it, and shrug off positive strokes. The resulting depletion makes the child needy, demanding, and reluctant or unable to give back much to anyone.

''. . . About four weeks after mother had died, Wendy complained that no one loved her. In an attempt to reassure her, her father named a long list of people who did (naming those who cared for her). On this Wendy commented aptly, 'But when my mommy wasn't dead I didn't need so many people—I needed just one' '' (Bowlby III, p. 280).

PROVOCATIVE CHILDREN

Each of us seems to have a quota of energy that we need and seek out. "Low-bucket" children, too often perceiving themselves as unable to get positive energy, focus instead upon generating negative exchanges.

This seems to result partly from the way most parents react to their children. Bob and Pat Wilson linger over Saturday morning coffee; their children are quietly watching cartoons in the adjacent family room. Do the Wilsons go and say to their children, "You guys are terrific! Thank you for being so thoughtful so that we can have some time to ourselves"? No. But if the children begin to squabble loudly over what channel to watch, one or both parents will probably join the fray. The Wilsons are teaching their children that it is much easier to get negative attention than positive. If you need something in your bucket, all you have to do is make your parent mad at you, which is not particularly difficult.

Rules the parents may have learned as children ("Don't brag," "Don't be conceited") compound the problem. A child losing a caretaker may feel guilt and shame, and need to counteract these feelings by saying positive things to himself, yet he cannot do so without breaking these ingrained parental rules. The child growing up in a family with adults who withhold positive attention or say primarily negative things to and about him has added difficulty, because he lacks a model to show him how to treat himself right. He has little idea of how to go about filling his own bucket with positive feelings.

As a result, many children react to a loss or sequential losses by provoking negative exchanges, constantly pushing and testing physical and verbal limits. Unfortunately, each negative interaction depletes more good feelings and starts the cycle over.

These children need help to stop the cycle of provocation and begin to interact in positive, bucket-filling ways. When someone other than the caretaker works with such a child, the best gains occur when the family is involved in helping enhance the child's sense of belonging, competence, and self-worth. The child needs caring and support; she needs to develop or renew feelings of meaning, predictability, self-esteem, and trust. But if her way of coping with a loss or separation results in difficult behavior, the parent is hard pressed to provide her with healing experiences. If their relationship is to be mutually pleasing, the parent must be involved in changing the child's perceptions of herself and others. Working with the child and caretaker together, you can help them to discover together how provocative behavior is learned and can be unlearned.

Teaching Positive Attention-Getting

Mrs. Martin is having trouble handling her nine-year-old daughter. She complains that Jenny is fresh, refuses to comply with simple requests to pick up her room or put away her laundry, threatens to run away. These threats often follow haranguing sessions; Mrs. Martin has found herself locked into "Did so" / "Did not" conversations that make her feel like a nine-year-old herself. Jenny and her mother come for counseling.

> HELPER: Wow, Jenny. It surely sounds as if you are good at making your mom upset. Is that true?
>
> JENNY: Yeah. [Grins.]
>
> HELPER: Let me check on that. Tell me, what are three things you can do for sure to get your mom mad at you?
>
> JENNY: I can be late for school and I can leave my clothes all over the floor and, I know, I can forget to feed the cat.
>
> HELPER: [To mother] Is she right about those? Okay. Now, Jenny, I want you to tell me three things you can do for sure to get a hug from your mom.
>
> JENNY: [Looking quite confused] Hunh?
>
> HELPER: What are three things you can do for sure to get a hug from your mom? [JENNY shrugs shoulders.]

HELPER: [Looking at mother] I think we've got part of the problem here. Jenny may need some help from you to figure this out.

MOTHER: [Genuinely surprised] Why Jenny, there are lots of ways you can get hugs!

HELPER: Tell her three.

MOTHER: You could pick up your room in the morning. And you could set the table without complaining. And you could say that you were sorry once in a while.

HELPER: What about it, Jenny, do you think those things might work? Okay. Which of those would be the easiest for you to do?

JENNY: Setting the table, probably.

Assigning Homework. You can help the child and parent agree on new behavior to practice during the coming week. In this case, Jenny will experiment with setting the table as an easy way to get hugs. Mrs. Martin will make sure that Jenny gets some positive attention for this change in behavior.

The homework must spell out clearly what is to be done. The parent may want to child to "be more affectionate"; that is too general. "How would I know that Jenny was being more affectionate? What would I see or hear that was different from what is happening now?" "Well, you'd see her give me a hug once in a while." "How many hugs would you like?" "One a day would be nice." At this point, make the assignment specifically, making sure both parent and child know what is requested. "Jenny, your mom is asking for a hug a day. Would that be hard or easy for you? Are you willing to try it and see if it helps stop the yelling?" As a rule of thumb, if you can't count what is requested, it probably isn't specific enough.

When homework is assigned, you will have to remember the assignment and check on it at the next session. In addition, check your notes to remember important details of information that has been shared, and arrive at sessions on time and ready to work. These are all ways of saying to parent and child, "You are important"—one good way of building self-esteem.

Practicing Positive Interaction

In this same session, or later, the helper might want to check with Jenny whether she likes hugs. As we have seen, some children become quite distrustful following a loss or a change of caretaker, and need a lot of space between themselves and others. The helper could say to Jenny, "Would you try something for me? Would you go over to your mom and stand beside her? Thank you." "Now, Mrs. Martin, will you give Jenny a good hug? Thank you. Okay, Jenny, now I need to ask you, did you like that?" Children who have difficulty with closeness will tell you plainly with words or physical expressions that they are uncomfortable. These children need homework that involves ten minutes or so of close time with their caretaker as a way of repairing their distrust of closeness.

If, however, the child likes the hug, you may intervene further. "Okay, you looked like that felt pretty good to you. I liked the way you hugged your mom back, and I bet she liked it too. Is that right, Mrs. Martin? Now, Jenny, I want to tell you an important secret that not all kids know. One of the ways you've been practicing getting hugs is by setting the table without complaining. But the secret is, anytime you want a hug *you can ask for one.* You can give a hug and get one back, or just say, 'Mom, I want a hug.' Will you try that for me now and see what happens?" In most cases, the beleaguered parent is only too glad to be asked for a positive interaction, and responds willingly to the request.

The ability to practice new behavior at a safe time and in a safe place is another strength of having a regular helper interact with the child. Moreover, the concept of practice is useful in itself, because it implies that nobody has to be immediately comfortable with or perfect at the new behavior. Children and parents need to be warned that new things take much practice, and that sometimes people will forget and fall back into doing things the old way; but initial attempts set the stage for starting over and trying again, which is essential in mastering a new way of interacting.

Jenny and her mother must be told that there may be some times when Jenny asks for a hug her mother cannot conveniently give. Encourage her mother to hug if she can, or to tell Jenny, "Not right now, but when I finish the paper [or drain the spaghetti, or finish this phone call]." This keeps Jenny from interpreting the answer as "No, not ever." The parent, of course, must keep the promise, or the message becomes "Positive doesn't work—try negative instead."

Helping the Child Make Choices

As these interventions produce more and more episodes of positive interaction, the child can be weaned away from seeking negative attention through provocative behavior. It is not easy to stop a habit unless there is something as good or better to substitute; but now the child can be confronted when he acts in a way that has negative results. Encourage the parent to say, "You are making this chore of picking up your room into a war. Which would you rather have right now, a hug or a fight?" Or, aware that the child is beginning to slide into old patterns, the parent can say, "I think you are acting like a kid that needs a hug, and I have one right here for you."

Provocative children and their parents seem to respond well to these methods, and patterns of conflict give way to a close, responsive give-and-take that makes everyone involved feel "high-bucket."

Using Praise to Restore Positive Self-Esteem

Praise is another bucket-filler, an interaction involving positive energy. The praise must be genuine, though; and you should make sure that the child is not discounting the positive energy directed her way, out of a sense of guilt or shame. Sometimes praise is brushed off verbally, sometimes shrugged off with the shoulders or a shake of the head. When this happens, confront the child. "I said something nice to you and you didn't believe it. How can I say it so you will?" Eye contact and physical contact with the child (cupping her chin, touching her knee, placing a hand on her shoulder) reinforces the verbal message.

Praising the child's developing competence is particularly beneficial: "You did a good job." "You made a good choice." "You are really getting better at that."

Helpers as well as caretakers can use praise with good results, especially when it involves good things said about the child by another adult: "The doctor said that you were a really strong baby." "Your dad told me that you were clever, and I believe him." This is a form of praise that seems to be hard for children to discount. When the adult says something complimentary about the child to another adult while the child listens, it has extra clout, because most children are under the impression that adults don't lie to one another.

It is also important to teach the child to praise himself. Sometimes this needs to be taught almost by rote: "What a beautiful picture you've drawn. You should feel really proud of yourself." "You did a really good job of cleaning up. You should feel good about yourself." In time you can begin to check to see if the child is incorporating similar patterns internally. "What a beautiful picture you've drawn. What should you say to yourself?" "I dunno." "What do I say to you?" "You say, 'You should feel good about it.'" "Well, do you?" "Yeah." "Terrific!"

Dealing with the Good–Bad Split in Children

It is not infrequent for two children in the same family to respond in quite different ways to their loss of or separation from a parent. One may seem to lock herself into the provocative "bad" child role, while the other, fearful of rocking the boat and driving the caretaker away, becomes "too good to be true." He may seem somewhat superficial and plastic, lacking normal feelings and reactions to life. Often he has trouble learning, and is unduly anxious about looking good, being right, not making mistakes. This anxiety may prevent him from trying new experiences, or make him feel inferior to other children, though he often assumes an outward posture of superiority and is quick to tattle or enjoy another's distress or mistake.

When siblings assume opposite ends of a good–bad split, the initial intervention frequently takes place with the provocative youngster. Interestingly enough, as the "bad" child begins to discover ways to get positive energy, the "goody two-shoes" sibling will experiment with negative interactions. Sometimes this involves instigating blowups from the provocative child by whispered taunts or hidden pokes. The caretaker should not assume that it is always the loud, provocative child who is at fault. More often, the "good" child, particularly if helped to own his feelings about the loss as discussed in Chapter 3, will begin to experiment with the very same negative behaviors that the provocative child has given up. It is as if the "good" child becomes certain that nothing terrible will result, for he has seen the caretaker remain available to his sister while she was acting bad.

You may be reluctant to work with the "good" child, for fear of rocking the boat or making a good child naughty. If you don't, though, chances are the child will continue to feel guilty and anxious, locked into unresolved sadness and anger. That is a great price to pay.

HELPLESSNESS AND HOPELESSNESS

Because children who suffer a loss or separation are usually unable to remedy the situation, they understandably have strong feelings of helplessness—they begin to think of themselves as weak, feeble, and powerless. These feelings are compounded if, through shame or guilt, the child begins to feel helpless about her ability to make and maintain close relationships. It may become even worse if, in the internal disorganization that normally follows a loss, the child finds herself unable to master important tasks such as learning new information at school, resettling in a new neighborhood, and making new friends— things that would previously have been well within her capability.

Some children respond to these feelings of helplessness by giving in to them. They feel powerless, incompetent, and inefficient; they make no attempt to tackle problems and work them out; and when they do experience success they discount it and credit it to luck, which is extremely damaging to their self-esteem. In some children this "learned helplessness," as Bowlby calls it, leads to what would be quickly diagnosed in an adult as a depressive disorder. These children admit to feeling low, sad, discouraged, and hopeless. They often show at least four of the following eight symptoms of depression: loss of appetite or weight, difficulty sleeping, fatigue, agitation or lethargy, loss of interest in things, difficulty concentrating, feelings of guilt, and wishing for death or thoughts of suicide. Simos points out that sleeping more than usual may also be a signal of withdrawal into hopelessness, as are hyperactivity, problems in peer relationships, poor academic performance, hypochondriasis or physical complaints, delinquency, fighting, vandalism, accident-proneness, and severe hand-banging or face-beating. The inability of a young person to fantasize about the future may be regarded as a warning sign of hopelessness or even of potential suicide (Simos p. 192).

If children fight their feelings of helplessness, they often do so in passive-aggressive ways. They may "dump" their feelings on the helper, for example, by asking for help but discounting any suggestions with a "yes, but . . ."—often so successfully that would-be helpers feel helpless too. Sometimes they follow up this externalization of their own helplessness by attacking, accusing the helper of being ineffective or unconcerned.

Children may also respond with a desire for complete control, of themselves and of others. The child who seems fearless while pumping himself on a swing panics on a merry-go-round, where he is not in control. He acts aggressive and/or over-competent in his relationships with others, as if he cannot count on adults but must take charge to keep himself safe. He tries to control everything in his environment, and has difficulty meeting even reasonable demands. No matter what limits are set on this child, he oversteps the boundaries, sending the messages, "I don't need you; I'll take care of myself," and "If I let you win control over me, I'll lose again." He is often a difficult patient for the person who has to administer a shot, examine his ears, or work on his teeth, for he is likely to fight back, terrified of being under the control of a powerful, hurtful adult.

Letting the child experience being in charge, being included in decision making, and exercising control over some areas of his life seems to work well with either of these responses to help-lessness. At the same time, of course, the caretaker must set limits when the child clearly demonstrates that he is not ready to assume responsibility for himself.

In helping a child recover from "learned helplessness" to more autonomous behavior, or relinquish some inappropriate and self-defeating attempts to control, the helper should under-stand what kinds of self-expression and self-determination are allowed this child by his family. Is the child allowed to do his own thinking? to make choices? Is the child allowed to disagree? Are things so bad, either because a bereaved caretaker is handling her own helplessness by being overly controlling or because she is trying to recover from a challenging child, that the parent now sees the child's every attempt to assert autonomy, appropriate or not, as a challenge, a war to be won? Which rules of the family are negotiable and which are not?

Problem-Solving with Negotiation

One way to give power to a child with "learned helplessness" or defuse a child's struggle for control is to use Dreikur's technique of mutual problem solving. Helper and child meet—with the parent, if the parent is not the helper—and deliberate solutions to their problem. Problem solving follows these steps:

1. Agree what is the problem. Be specific; for example, evenings are spent fighting about whether it is time for the child to get ready for bed, instead of doing things together.

2. Brainstorm. Parents and children throw out any ideas that occur to them on how this problem might be solved. Write these down. No one is allowed to comment or react to any suggestion until this step is completed. This lets parents and children pull together on the same side to defeat the problem, engendering a

sense of teamwork. It defuses the conflict of "your way" and "my way," which may be the first two suggestions on the list, and allows parents and children to think of new solutions that may have been overlooked in their struggle for power.

3. Discuss each item on the list. If someone questions whether a suggested solution might work, make a question mark in the margin. If anyone feels that a suggested solution might harm him in some way, cross out the suggestion. Usually this leaves one or two suggestions, which may or may not have a question mark.

4. Take a vote on the remaining suggestions to see which is preferred; it will be tried first. If someone questions one of the solutions, brainstorm some more or simply discuss ways to eliminate the concern.

5. When an agreement is reached, set a time period (often one week) to experiment with the solution.

6. Ask participants if they can foresee any way that they might sabotage the trial solution. Make sure they agree to do their part in trying to makethe solution work.

At the end of the trial period, participants come together to evaluate how the proposed solution has worked. At that time they may discover that it has solved the problem, and agree to continue with it; or they may discover that the solution has solved parts of the problem but aggravated others, or that the solution has not worked—at which point they begin again.

This technique works surprisingly well. Each person feels as if he has won and no one has lost. The session between parent and child has begun with a problem and ended on a positive, cooperative note, leaving both with energy to work on the proposed change.

Occasionally, the brainstorming will produce no solution agreeable to everyone. The helper can then say, "Well, it looks as if this problem is still smarter than we are. Let's give ourselves a week to see if we can't come up with something to beat it." The following week the technique can be used again. Sometimes, too, a child who is feeling helpless will be reluctant to involve herself in the process at all. She may mumble, talk softly, use incomplete sentences, and say "I don't know," or "I don't care." Such a child should be encouraged to use her energy and power: "When you say that, you give away all your power and then everybody bosses you. How about holding on to that power and being your own boss?"

Non-Negotiable Rules and Decisions

If the child is being given a chance to make decisions and to control parts of his life, it becomes much easier for him to accept authority in other parts. Caretakers can make it clear that there are some areas where the child has no choice. But even this can be done in ways that allow him some freedom while setting firm limits.

Giving the child choices with logical consequences is one way. "You must do your homework. I can't say yes to your going to the movies tomorrow unless all your homework is finished. You may decide whether you want to do it now and have time for the movies tomorrow, or whether you will decide to do it tomorrow instead of going to the movies."

Giving the child two or more good choices is another way. "I know you would like to stay and play, but it is time to go. That is not your choice. Your choice is to decide: do you want to walk to the car, skip to the car, or have me carry you?"

Each of these methods sets the stage for the caretaker or helper to encourage the child's self-esteem. "I like the way you took care of that homework so that you could go to the movies. Good choice." "It's fun watching how well you skipped to the car. Good work."

When the child lapses into old behavior, the caretaker or helper can point out, without controlling, that the choice may not work out well, by merely asking, "Is that a good choice or a bad one? Will it work out for you or not?" Using these approaches means that the child will sometimes make a bad choice; then the consequences must follow, or further negotiation must occur. Children need to be told, "Everyone makes mistakes. The important thing about this is, what did you learn and how can you fix it?"

If the child who is given two choices tries to add an unacceptable one, the caretaker or helper should remind her, "That is not one of your choices; your choices are [name them]. Which would you like to choose?" Remember that the goal is to help the child make choices that work out well for her, not to take control of the child.

Helping the Child Experience Self-Control

With both the child who gives away his power and the one who is overly controlling, there are ways to provide experiences that promote self-esteem and help the child take and relinquish responsibility more effectively. These methods have the added benefit of allowing the child to take and relinquish control under the direction of the adult. One thing that the child can control easily, for example, is his own breathing. You can play a game in which you ask him to close his eyes and concentrate on his own breathing until he can feel and hear it. He can experiment with holding and releasing his breath, with raising and lowering some part of his body in time to his breathing, and with breathing at different tempos. All these activities are totally under the child's control, and help him understand that he is capable of controlling himself.

Other useful activities include start–stop games such as "Captain [or Mother], May I," in which the child takes turns directing and being directed in what steps are allowed; or the statue-making game, where child and adult take turns spinning the other around and then dropping into a position and holding it. You might ask the child to lean as far forward as possible before he falls to the ground or puts his foot out to regain his balance. Such playful experiences of his own physical self-control help the child to learn that he can make choices regarding his own physical behavior in other arenas as well —such as the choice to stop doing something particularly disruptive.

Redefining Use of Yes and No

Fatigued from a constant battle with the child, a caretaker may overlook some of the positive aspects of a child's self-determination. I sometimes respond to a parent's litany of complaints like this: "It certainly sounds as if Carol is good at saying no." "Boy, you can say that again." "You know, that's a real strength. Imagine how concerned you'd be if she got to be thirteen or fourteen and couldn't do it." "Oh." "The thing we have to work on now is helping her understand how to use the power of her 'no' in a way that works well for her." Parents can also be helped to see that it takes more self-esteem to say no than to be always compliant.

You might tell children who have trouble following parental "no's" and are easily led by other children that they are choosing not to use a talent.For example:

> HELPER: So even though your mother told you not to go over to that empty building to play, you and Leon went anyway. I'm wondering why you made that choice when you knew your mom would be really mad.
>
> STEPHEN: Well, Leon made me.
>
> HELPER: He did? How did he do that? Did he pick you up and carry you there?
>
> STEPHEN: No, but he called me chicken.
>
> HELPER: He called you chicken and then you had to go?
>
> STEPHEN: Yeah!
>
> HELPER: Does that always work for you? Anybody can get you to do what they want by calling you a chicken? Your head is saying yes and your shoulders are saying you're not sure. Let me check it out. What if Lisa [his older sister] decided that she didn't want to do the dishes when it was her turn. Maybe what she could do then would be to point a finger at you and say, "Stephen, I bet you are too chicken to do these dishes. Chicken, chicken, chicken!" Then would you have to do the dishes?
>
> STEPHEN: No way!

> HELPER: I guess that "chicken" power is something you know how to say no to. Let's see what you know about saying no to Lisa when she uses it and not saying no to Leon when he does.

Sometimes it helps to encourage the rebellious strength in a youngster, if that is where the available energy is. The child can be urged to prove his value by "showing them" how well he can do in life.

Children, and adolescents in particular, may need to be helped to see that there can be power in saying yes as well as in saying no. "Ginny, I hear you saying 'no way' to most everything in your life right now. You don't want to follow the rules at home, you don't want to be in school, you don't want to get a job. I know what you don't want; now I'm interested in what you do want. If you could make a plan for yourself, what would you decide to say yes to?"

Over-Anxiety and Competence

Some children try to ward off feelings of helplessness and hold on to their sense of self-esteem by becoming unusually concerned with keeping themselves safe. Anna Freud suggests that children separated from their mothers may tend to take over the mothering role themselves by taking good care of their own bodies, thereby holding on to their infant experiences of being in the lost mother's care.

Some such children exhibit anxiety about personal safety. One child who was asked, "If you could be any kind of animal at all, what would you be," responded, "Well, I wouldn't want to be a bull because they put you in bullfights and stick you with swords. And I certainly wouldn't want to be a pig because I'd end up pork chops in someone's freezer. And I wouldn't want to be a bug because someone would smash me. And I wouldn't want to be a bird because someone might shoot me. How about lizards, do they live a long time? I guess I might be a lizard like the kind that changes, a chameleon, because then I could hide wherever I was and no one could hurt me."

Other children become afraid to relinquish their own control even slightly for fear something terrible will happen. Children like this are often helped by being praised for their efforts in their own behalf ("I like how you take care of yourself"), and helped to feel competent in doing so ("You make good choices"). When they express a fear or concern, it helps if you listen thoughtfully and give concrete information if it is available to counteract the fear, rather than just brushing it aside.

Another way to help such children is to teach them to take care of themselves, not in ways that push them to take on responsibility before they are ready, but in ways to help them feel that they can play a part in caring for themselves. For instance, because there is such a close connection between nurturing and feeding, the child who becomes a competent cook often feels that if the chips were down at least she wouldn't starve to death. Even very young children can be taught to make a sandwich or fix a bowl of cereal. Slightly older children can learn to cook eggs, pancakes, hot dogs, or other simple dishes as soon as they are tall enough to use a stove safely.

It also helps to let the child know that she can take care of her needs for safety and nurturing. When she says, "Mom, I need a hug," you can say, "I like to hug you and I like the way you ask for what you want." You can initiate conversations that make the child feel secure in her ability to get help if the caretaker is not present. Adult: "What would you do if we lost each other at the grocery store?" Child: "I'd ask someone to help me find you." "What would you do if you got home from school and I was late?" "I'd go to [place] or call [person]," rehearsing whatever has been arranged between you. These children, more than others, need to sense that they know what to do in an emergency.

Obviously, if you have a fearful child you should not make him anxious about calamities or give him other new things to worry about. Rather, address concerns following clues from the child as to what worries him. To ensure personal safety, however, all children need certain kinds of information sooner or later: how to call the operator, how to report an emergency, how to respond in case of fire. Often conversations will result from discussions at school or in scouts, or from something heard on the news or read in the paper. At these times, children need clear information about how to protect themselves, and they need to be told, "I like how you are figuring out how to take good care of yourself."

Coming to Grips with Impotency

Finally, children have to come to grips with the fact that there are areas in their lives where they have no choices and no impact. Decisions about which adults will care for the child are out of his control; so is the possibility of reunion with a caretaker following death or, often, separation. The child may need help maintaining positive self-esteem and power while recognizing that in some areas he is or was helpless.

Part of the support he needs comes from caretakers who appreciate the child's developing capabilities to think, to feel, to solve problems, to do good work, to make good choices. Other times a helper can gently encourage the child to let go of fantasies about how he might make things work out differently, respecting his desires for a different ending but pointing out his limitations in effecting it.

This was necessary, for example, with Shawn, who had come into the foster care system at age four as a result of severe neglect by alcoholic parents. Seen at nine, Shawn was still wrestling with his wishes to return to his parents. "I'm older now," he argued. "I can take care of myself." "That's partly true," the helper said. "But what could you do if no one was working to earn money for your food and electricity?" "I'd just get a job." At this point Shawn could have been told forcefully that he needed to be in school, that it was his job to work at growing up and not to worry about taking care of his parents, that nine-year-olds can't get jobs, that the law said he had to be in school. But this approach would not meet the child where he is, and would only drive his fantasies underground. The helper chose to follow Shawn's line of thought instead.

"You know, that is an interesting idea," she said. "Maybe if you had gotten a job in the first place you would still be at home, what do you think?" "Yeah." "Let's see, imagine it with me. There you are a fine little boy about this tall. You wake up in the morning and you're hungry, but you can't find anything to eat. Your parents are both sound asleep. You are tired of being hungry and you decide that what you will do is get a job. You look for your clothes; what do you think you might wear?" "I know, my red corduroy overalls!" "Sounds good to me. Gee, Shawn, do you think you knew how to button when you were four?" (This question gently begins to establish some reality.) "Okay, now your shoes. What about it, could you tie your shoes when you were four? Well, never mind, they'll probably give you a job even if you just tuck the shoelaces into your shoes. Okay, now let's go down the stairs and out the door. You live on a pretty busy street; we'd better cross at the light up there at the corner. While we're waiting for the light to turn green—you think you know about not crossing with red lights?—let's see what kind of a job you're looking for." Shawn, who was either a smart nine-year-old or had been giving this some thought, volunteered that he thought he could get work in a filling station or else bagging groceries. "Okay, there's the green light and there's a filling station just across the street. Why don't you ask the man for a job?" "Hey, Mister, I need a job," Shawn said. " 'Well, that's swell, because I need someone to work for me.' " Shawn's eyes grew bigger. "Just then along comes another grownup, and he asks for a job too." Shawn's face fell. "The man at the gas station says, 'I'm sorry, son, but I think maybe you are too short to wash the windshields.' " Shawn piped up, "I'd just get on the hood of the car and show him." "You know, I bet you could do a good job of that, too," his helper said. "The trouble is that even if he wanted to hire you, he couldn't. There is a law that says that kids your age have to be in school and they can't get jobs like that." "Well, I hate that dumb law." "I can see that. But what can you do about it? Maybe when you are a grownup you will want to try to get them to change it. But right now I think you are stuck."

By entering into the child's fantasy and gently and supportively leading to the question "but what can you do about it?" the helper shows that the wish is unrealistic, yet encourages retention of self-esteem even while recognizing helplessness in the here and now. To add that the child may one day have the power to fix what prevents his hoped-for ending also helps him to accept the current situation without relinquishing all hope.

6.
Letting Go
and Moving On

BECAUSE EVERY MAJOR LOSS disrupts the development of self-esteem, the smooth progression of life, and the sense that events are predictable and meaningful, recovery from such a loss requires that damaged self-esteem be repaired, continuity be reestablished, and a sense of meaning be restored. To recover as fully as possible from a loss, a child must satisfy five needs.

First, the child must understand that he was born to a mother and father; he must know who they were, why he was separated from one or both of them (without blaming himself for the separation), and what, if anything, he might do to return things to their previous condition. He must experience and share any strong feelings of anger, sadness, guilt, or shame that he has been holding back.

Second, the child must know what persons or families have cared for him if he has lived away from his birth parents. Who are the people in these places he has lived, why did he go to those places, why did he leave (or why will he be leaving), and what, if anything, might he have done to make things work out differently?

Third, the child must say goodbye, directly or symbolically, to past caretakers (and, if a change of caretaker is forthcoming, he must say hello to the new caretaker).

Fourth, the child must receive permission from his caretakers to be happy, loved, successful, and loving.

Fifth, the child must get ready to face the future with increasingly diminishing concern about the past.

We have discussed techniques to help satisfy the first two needs in previous chapters. In this chapter we will look at ways to help children say goodbye, let go, and move on.

Saying Goodbye

Certain kinds of losses can be anticipated—separation and divorce, hospitalization, incarceration, absence because of business or military service, the impending death of a family member—and it is always easier to handle any loss if it is expected and planned for.

For many children, even a gradual loss involves a complete separation from their families, friends, and environment. The child who must move from one custodial situation to another —whether as a result of parental remarriage, foster care, a visit to a distant parent, or even placement in day care—will be helped by careful planning at all stages of the move. There must be time to prepare for the change; to say goodbye to the old caretaker and hello to the new one; and to express feelings of sadness, anger, rejection, and anxiety with support from both families and other adults.

If a parent will be moving away, the child who is included in discussions about the move can be reassured that the parent will continue to care. She can express her strong feelings and put to rest the thought that her parent is leaving because of something she did, wished, or felt. If there is to be a change of caretaker, the child who is forewarned of the change is given a chance to anticipate where she will live and who will keep her safe. If illness or injury may result in death to a family member, the child who is given appropriate information has a chance to say direct goodbyes to the dying relative. Children in these situations seem most able to come to grips with the reality of their loss and to find some peace in having said goodbye to what was before it was completely lost.

Other children, however, are victims of either a sudden, unexpected loss or a separation that may be only temporary. Or they have been moved so quickly that no time has been allowed for a shared goodbye. These children find accepting the loss and their feelings about it much more difficult. They need a chance to say their goodbyes in whatever way is possible. Perhaps such a child can say goodbye during a funeral or memorial service or a visit to the grave site. Perhaps she can visit with the non-custodial caretaker and talk the situation over, saying goodbye to what has been but gaining reassurance that caring will continue even if there is to be no visiting. Perhaps the absent caretaker can be encouraged to write a letter or make a tape for the child, explaining that he or she will no longer provide daily nurture, wishing the child well, and saying goodbye. If a child has had multiple caretakers, the helper may find it useful to contact these individuals and ask them to write or tape a message of goodbye and good wishes or to visit with the child so that goodbyes can be shared. Any of these experiences can help a child complete her understanding of the changes in her life so that she can move on to new relationships with her self-esteem intact while continuing to care deeply about the lost family member.

Occasionally a child must say goodbye symbolically. A caretaker who has disappeared or is unwilling to communicate with the child about events leading up to the separation cannot wish the child well or say goodbye. In this event a helping adult can intervene in a number of ways. The helper can encourage the child to write a letter, to be sent to the former caretaker or shared with others, as a means of unloading wishes and feelings. If the parent is dead, this letter could be read at the grave site. Or the letter might be read aloud to other important people in the child's life. Role playing could include the child's pretending to call the absent caretaker on a play phone to express feelings and say goodbye. The child could be asked to visualize the absent caretaker sitting in the room and to have a conversation with him or her. Play figures might be used to act out a meeting, a goodbye conversation, and a parting. The helper can initiate one of these activities by saying something like, "When you stopped living with your mom you never really had a chance to say goodbye to her. You've been thinking about her a lot, and it seems to me as if you are ready to say goodbye to her as the parent you live with. That doesn't mean you'll ever stop loving her, it just means you'll say goodbye to living with her while you are growing up. If you could call her up [or write her a letter or talk to her] today, what kinds of things would you like to say to her?" After the child has responded the helper can ask what the child would hope that the mother might say in return and if the child is afraid something bad might happen.

The helper must be certain, of course, that enough time has elapsed for the process of grieving to have been completed except for this final step. Studies of widows have shown that a majority take two to three years to stabilize their lives, to overcome their preoccupation with yearning and searching, to relinquish hope that things will return to how they used to be, and to accept the finality of their loss. "Regardless of how effectively grieving is done, it cannot be collapsed in time," Simos tells us. "Events such as birthdays, anniversaries, and other important dates are associated with that which has been lost and these calendar events must be experienced at least once after the loss before the bereaved can feel the pain of living through the event without that which he has lost. It takes, therefore, at least a year before each of these calendar-related events can be lived through" (p. 41). Surely, symbolic goodbyes should be delayed until this year is over to be certain that the child is ready for them. (Actual goodbyes to the departing caretaker should be said before and at the time of loss, if possible, and anytime thereafter without waiting for the year to pass.)

Anniversary Reaction

A great many children who have experienced loss or separation find the holidays a difficult time, often for years afterwards. For some a particular holiday is difficult; for others a particular season or month triggers a recurrence of yearning and sadness. In children who were very small at the time of the loss, this reaction may be triggered by the lengthening or shortening of the day as the seasons change. The anniversary reaction is particularly evident when the loss is associated with a change into or out of daylight-saving time. Like other living creatures, children seem to keep track of the seasons with these light changes, and their grief may recycle in accordance with them. Recycling may include particular forms of behavior displayed at the time of loss, such as an increase or decrease in appetite, activity, aggression, or self-control, as well as sadness, discouragement, and yearning.

Wishes for What Might Have Been

Many children remain bound to an absent caretaker by their wishes about what might have been. These powerful wishes, which follow many people well into their adult years, are found not only in those of us who lost a caretaker as children but also in those who yearned to get something from our parents that they were unable or unwilling to give us. This useful exercise clarifies unfulfilled wishes, encourages acceptance of the inability to make such wishes come true, and focuses on ways to satisfy longings. "Once upon a time there was a little girl [or boy] who really wished her mom [or dad, or both] would . . . . That would have been good for her because . . . . Instead she got a mom [or dad, or both] who . . . . That was bad for her because . . . . She tried everything she knew." (If an older child, adolescent, or adult is doing the exercise, you might want to have them list what they tried.) "But nothing worked. Now she is deciding to get what she wants by . . . ."

Lifting Curses

Some children and adolescents (and some adults) grieve for years because of a curse, either self-pronounced or unintentionally inflicted by a caretaker. These persons may act out their curse over and over. Most self-pronounced curses result from the magical thinking described in Chapter 1. Other curses are said in anger by one or more caretakers: "You'll be the death of me yet." "You'll drive me crazy." "You'll never make it." "Who could love a kid like you?"

Obviously, the best way to lift these curses is to get the person or persons who gave them to take them back. The child who is helped to understand the adult reasons behind his loss or separation is freed from his self-inflicted curse. A former caretaker can modify or take back an accusation in a revisit or goodbye message, particularly if the adult is alerted to the child's feelings.

Sometimes, however, the curse needs to be lifted in other ways. One way is for the helper to use the power of wishes by saying clearly and repeatedly, "I'll be glad when you can stop thinking that there is something wrong about you." Or a child can be helped through symbolic play to undo a curse. Raoul, who left a foster home suddenly after four years, struggled to overcome his sadness and anger at his foster mother for some time. He was able to release enough of his feelings that he began to progress again in school and enjoy his new foster parents. But his previous foster mother's anger haunted him. He continued to see himself as a burden. In a play session he was asked if he would like to pretend to call her up and apologize for the crisis that had precipitated his move.

RAOUL [using play telephone]: Hello, Ma?
HELPER: Yeah, this is me.
RAOUL: I wanted to say I'm sorry about what happened. I wanted to say I have another family and I am doing okay.
HELPER: That's good. I wondered about you and how you were doing. I know you're gonna do just fine 'cause you're a good boy a lot of the time, just not when you get so mad. I

hope you'll do good there 'cause I think you can. I hope you'll like it, too.

RAOUL: Yeah, well, it's okay here.

HELPER: That's real good.

RAOUL: That's all I got to say.

HELPER: Okay, goodbye.

RAOUL: Goodbye.

With Ronnie another technique was used. During one play session Ronnie set up the blocks as a house and put a mother doll and three girl dolls inside. This reflected Ronnie's personal history: when he had come into protective service for abuse and neglect his mother had appeared relieved to sign his relinquishment papers, but she had kept his three sisters. Four years after his adoption into a very supportive, sensitive family, Ronnie still struggled with his feelings that his mother thought he was worthless and threw him away but kept his sisters. During the play session Ronnie walked the small boy doll to the door of the house he had built. He made the boy doll knock on the door and the mother doll answer. "Hello," said the boy. "I'm your tiny boy, Ronnie." "Ronnie who?" asked the mother doll, slamming the door in his face.

The helper responded, "It might go like that. Let me show you another way it might be." She walked the boy doll up to the door and repeated Ronnie's greeting: "Hello, I'm your tiny boy, Ronnie." "Oh, Ronnie," said the mother doll, "look how you've grown! I must have made a good plan to help you find a family with a mom that knows how to take care of boys. It was really hard for me. I'm glad you got what you needed. Goodbye." Ronnie's face grew thoughtful. Within the next two weeks his posture improved, his behavior became less provocative, and his displays of tension became less frequent.

How Additional Losses Recycle Grief

As Bowlby points out, a number of situations other than family reunions and holidays may cause someone to experience recycled or delayed grief:

1. An anniversary of a death that has not been completely mourned or a separation that has not been resolved. This is often seen in older adopted children who begin to grieve after they have been in their new family about a year.

2. Another loss, apparently minor. This is evident but sometimes confused by the observing helper in two common situations. The first is a temper tantrum, which is often triggered by the loss or breakage of an object or a sense of helplessness. The second is the period of adolescence when the growing youngster experiences one loss after another—loss of friends as they outgrow one another, loss of elementary school and teachers, loss of boyfriend or girlfriend, loss of innocence, loss of comfort with dependency at just the time when life is making extra demands. Many adolescents recycle grief as school graduation, with all the losses it involves, approaches. At these times not only do the current losses precipitate anniversary grief, but also the yearning for the comfort and support of an absent parent increases.

3. Reaching the age that a parent had been when he or she died.

4. A loss suffered by another with whom the mourner strongly identifies and for whom the mourner provides encompassing care (Bowlby III, p. 158).

Children may be vulnerable to recycled or delayed grief at other times, such as when a parent remarries or an adoption is due to be finalized. It seems that at those times the part of the child that has been hoping for a reunion against all reason is forced to acknowledge that what has been in the past is really, permanently over.

Helping Establish Bonds with New Caretakers

There is no question that substitution of one caretaker for another can be vitally important in a child's attempt to reestablish continuity, sense of meaning, and self-esteem. But, as Freud points out, no matter what may fill the gap left by a loss, even if it is filled completely, what is lost cannot be restored

(Bowlby III, p. 23). Even though searching and yearning may cease to be a major preoccupation, yearning never ends. The absent parent's nurture can be relinquished because in fact it is never completely given up but kept inside, where it often leads the child to adopt traits, tastes, values, interests, symptoms, illnesses, or other attributes of the parent. This is of great practical importance, especially when a bereaved child is expected to establish a relationship with a new caretaker. The success of the new relationship does not depend on the fading of the memory of the earlier one; rather, the more distinct the two relationships are kept, the more the new one is likely to prosper.

A child may feel conflicting loyalties if he thinks he must turn his back on his old caretaker before he can share affection and intimacy with a new one. The helping adult must respect the child's need to maintain ties to a noncustodial parent while devising ways to help the child understand that you can have a parent-child relationship with more than one parent or set of parents. One helpful technique is the candle ritual described in Chapter 1 of this book. As the child lights a new candle for each caretaker in her life, she can see vividly that the love and warmth she felt with earlier caretakers does not have to be "blown out" as new bonds are established, new candles lit. Variations of this ceremony can be used with foster children, children who are being adopted, and stepchildren who are worried that if they have to share their parent with a stepbrother or stepsister they will somehow lose their parent's love. The ceremony shows in a way that even the youngest children understand that new family constellations do not demand the death of old relationships, and that differences between family members can be tolerated.

ENDING THE WORK

Healthy mourning, according to Anna Freud, is achieved when a person accepts the changes in his external life, makes corresponding changes in his internal life, and finally makes the reorientation necessary to be able to feel attachment again.

When children resolve their grief, additionally, they often set new goals for themselves and sometimes adopt new values. Self-esteem damaged by the loss is restored, and the new self is enriched by the memories of that which has been lost as well as by a sense of growth through suffering and mastery of grief. Some children feel that the experience happened for the best, perhaps to teach them a valuable lesson. Many feel in subsequent years that their loss opened them to a fuller appreciation of life.

Separation from the Helper

If you help a child who is not your own through this important experience, you will probably become a trusted friend and source of support. Because the child has only recently resolved one loss, the helper who is not a parent must be sensitive to the child's vulnerability when terminating their relationship. Like any loss, separation from the helper should be expected and gradual, should not leave the child (or the child's caretaker) feeling helpless but should be planned with the child's participation, should allow the child to express any sadness and anger that he feels at the parting, should enhance the child's self-esteem, and should leave the child feeling strong and confident about his ability to cope without regular support from the helping adult.

When you feel that the child is ready, you can propose less frequent meetings as a kind of reward. "You have really been working hard for quite a time. You have earned a vacation —some time off to do what you want to do, to just have fun. I think what we should do for a while is see each other one week and then give you a vacation the next. How does that sound to you?" Or, with a younger child whose sense of time is incompletely developed: "I think you should have more time between our meetings for spending with your mom and playing, instead of having to make this long drive so often."

This message should convey your confidence that the child will find other useful and interesting things to do and that nothing bad will happen if the child misses a meeting. You should allow the child to resist or object. If the child objects strongly, you may want to ask him how many more times he feels you need to meet weekly before he will be ready to reduce the frequency of your meetings. Usually, if the child has resolved most of his conflicting feelings over the loss, he will readily—sometimes eagerly—accept the idea of meeting less often.

After a month or six weeks the child and her caretaker will both recognize that things are running smoothly without more frequent meetings. They may feel proud of how well they are managing; this feeling should be encouraged. Both caretaker and child will grow in self-confidence when they know they can manage well on their own. Occasionally old disputes or misbehaviors will be repeated, signaling that the child's problems may not be as close to resolution as you have judged them to be.

If things are going well, you may want to space the meetings to a month apart after completing whatever schedule was agreed to initially. ("We'll try meeting every other time for a month and then see how things are going.") The first meeting after a month's interval is often a goodbye meeting.

You may wish to give the child more say in planning the termination. "We've been meeting every other week for a while now and I think you're doing swell on your own. It looks like it's almost time to say goodbye to your coming here for a while. How many turns do you think you'll need to get ready to say goodbye?" Frequently children answer realistically that they will need one, two, or three more turns. Sometimes they ask for forty more turns, or some other large number; the helper must then explore their needs further. It is difficult for most of us to say goodbye to someone who is important to us; children often try to avoid this difficulty by replying, "I don't need any more turns. I'll just stop today." This is not a good plan because it does not allow the child to ready herself for an impending separation by making internal and external adjustments—by dealing with her feelings, and turning to alternative means of support.

As the helping adult you must be sure that the child does not harbor any suspicion that the termination is due to some wrong he has committed; he must understand that it truly results from his success in overcoming his difficulties.

Sometime during the final sessions it is useful for you to review for the child, and often for the child's caretaker, just what you have accomplished together. This allows the child to take credit for the tasks he has completed and the growing he has done. It is a pleasant way of "making sense of what we've done" and a further reinforcement of the child's sense of mastery and self-esteem. You should commend "the good choice of coming here and working hard" to remove any lingering feelings of inadequacy because help was needed. With an adolescent or a child able to do hypothetical reasoning, you might also explore the question, "What do you want to leave behind you here and what do you want to take with you as you leave?"

The Final Meeting

The helping adult and child frequently come together for their final meeting with feelings of pride and joy combined with sadness at the parting. Often it is helpful to the child if the adult expresses these mixed feelings: "When I thought about seeing you for the last time I wanted to shout how fantastic it was that you've done such great work that you won't need to be coming anymore, but at the same time I was really feeling how much I'm going to miss you, too."

It is often true that both helping adult and child will want to reserve the possibility of future meetings or an ongoing relationship, even if that will involve only memory. "You know that if you ever get mixed up about something that you and your dad can't figure out, I'll hope that we can work on it—all three of us?" "You have my phone number [or address], and if you ever want to check in I'll be glad to hear from you." "I'll never forget you." (Children often return for help twelve to twenty months after the original work has been completed, when one of life's stresses triggers a new problem. Such problems are often resolved in only two or three sessions; the child and the helper know each other so well that they are able to get things sorted out quickly.)

You may want to give the child a "graduation" gift or a written message of good wishes as something tangible to take away from your final session. The child may also wish to leave a note or present behind to assure herself that she will not be forgotten. Some helping adults treat the final session as a party and serve refreshments.

As the meeting closes, you may want to ask the child, "How do you want to say goodbye-for-now?" Whether or not they have had much physical contact with the helper, the majority of children want a good, strong hug, even though they may have difficulty asking for it. This often feels like a good way of parting to the adult, too. Finally, the helper should tell the child, "Thank you for being my friend. I've learned a lot from you. Take care of yourself." And the shared work comes to an end.

Ending Grief Work as a Parent

If you are the child's parent and have been helping him through the grieving period, there will probably be no clear ending to signify your child's passage from active grief into resolved grief. As you give your child time, allow for his own internal drive for health, and use the approaches we have discussed to help him move on when he founders, the child will gradually put the major struggles of grieving behind him and will focus his psychological energy on different tasks of growing up. You may notice particular milestones in his recovery process. Or there may be no outstanding changes, but rather a steady progress to the point where you recognize that he is functioning well.

The task that seemed so overwhelming and confusing in the beginning has unfolded in logical and understandable ways. Even if some grieving remains to be done, you feel more confident in helping the child through it using the skills and information you have learned. You may also feel that you and your child are more in tune with one another, more tolerant of your differences, and more secure in your mutual ability to reach out to each other and be met with understanding. By sharing a loss and working through it together your ties have been strengthened, your wounds healed. You, too, can now move on to other concerns and interests with a sense of a job well done and some pride in your own willingness to have helped your child through a difficult time.

Bibliography

Anderson, Leone C. 1979. *It's O.K. to cry*. Elgin, Illinois: The Child's World.

Bandler, Richard; Grinder, John; and Satir, Virginia. 1976. *Changing with families*. Palo Alto, Cal.: Science and Behavior Books, Inc.

Bettelheim, Bruno. 1950. *Love is not enough*. New York: Macmillan.

Bowlby, John. 1969, 1973, 1980. *Attachment and loss*, Volumes I-III. London: Hogarth Press.

Burke, Noreen Conroy, and Burke, Robert. 1979. *Young and in foster care*. Baldwin, N.Y.: Burke and Conroy Associates.

Colgrove, Melba; Bloomfield, Harold; and McWilliams, Peter. 1977. *How to survive the loss of a love*. New York: Bantam Books.

Dreikurs, Rudolf. 1974. *Family council*. Chicago: Henry Regnery.

Grollman, Earl A. 1967. *Explaining death to children*. Boston: Beacon Press.

Grollman, Earl A. 1975. *Talking about divorce*. Boston: Beacon Press.

Ilg, Frances L., and Ames, Louise Bates. 1955. *Child behavior*. New York: Harper & Brothers.

Jewett, Claudia L. 1978. *Adopting the older child*. Harvard, Mass.: Harvard Common Press.

Looff, David H. 1976. *Getting to know the troubled child*. Knoxville: University of Tennessee Press.

Oaklander, Violet. 1978. *Windows to our children*. Moab, Utah: Real People Press.

Pothier, Patricia. 1976. *Mental health counseling with children*. Boston: Little, Brown.

Simos, Bertha G. 1979. *A time to grieve*. New York: Family Service Association of America.

Sinberg, Janet. 1978. *Divorce is a grown-up problem*. New York: Avon.

Stuart, Irving R., and Abt, Lawrence Edwin. 1981. *Children of separation and divorce: management and treatment*. New York: Van Nostrand and Reinhold.

Index